GROWING UP AFRICAN IN AUSTRALIA

EDITED BY
MAXINE BENEBA CLARKE
WITH AHMED YUSSUF AND MAGAN MAGAN

Black Inc.

Published by Black Inc.,
an imprint of Schwartz Publishing Pty Ltd
Level 1, 221 Drummond Street
Carlton VIC 3053, Australia
enquiries@blackincbooks.com
www.blackincbooks.com

9781760640934 (paperback)
9781743820872 (ebook)

Cover design by Kim Ferguson
Cover images © Louise Whelan
Text design by Thomas Deverall and Akiko Chan
Typesetting by Akiko Chan

Printed in Australia by McPherson's Printing Group.

Contents

THE PLAYGROUND

WELCOME TO AUSTRALIA

THE BODY

CHANGEMAKERS

DHAQAN CELIS

For Africa, where we originated.

For Australia, our home.

Introduction

Maxine Beneba Clarke

African-diaspora Australians are settlers, albeit black-bodied, on black land – Aboriginal land – of which sovereignty has never been ceded. For all the othering and discrimination faced by African-diaspora Australians in the current climate, there is no escaping the perhaps uncomfortable reality that we, the colonised, are sometimes also we, the colonisers. Any discussion of blackness in an Australian context must be set against the history of this truth: we, too, are settlers here.

Despite what the anti-immigration rhetoric of successive Australian governments would have us believe, African-diaspora Australians are not a recent phenomenon. Coins belonging to the medieval Kilwa Sultanate in East Africa have been found on the Wessel Islands, indicating trade with Africa as far back as the twelfth century. The first recorded African-diaspora settlers were black convicts, eleven in number, transported by the British, on the First Fleet of 1788.

On their release, many bought land and brought up families in the area of Pennant Hills in western Sydney. Over time, because of its inhabitants of colour, the area became known to white settlers as 'Dixieland', named after the area of America's Lower South that incorporated Mississippi, Alabama, Louisiana and four other states of the slave belt (which were soon joined by four states of the Upper South) and made up the Confederate States of America from 1861 to 1865.

Though Ned Kelly is Australia's most infamous bushranger, one of the African arrivals on the First Fleet was Australia's first: the lesser known John Caesar, also known as Black Caesar. History still cannot pin down his place of birth. Madagascar or the West Indies, so it was heard. John Caesar became a servant in the parish of St Paul, in Deptford, England. According to transcript, he stole 240 shillings and thus arrived in the penal colony of New South Wales, on the *Alexander*. Black Caesar was a giant of a man. To eat beyond meagre rations, he stole. His life was a litany of thefts, captures, escapes and re-offences. Eventually, he formed a gang of men who became Australia's first known bushrangers.

In addition to suffering some of the degradations brought about by their dark complexions, early arrivals of African descent actively participated in the colonial project, and Black Caesar was no exception, most notably becoming involved in a shameful fight with Aboriginal warrior Pemulwuy.

Then there's William Blue – Billy Blue – who hailed from Jamaica: either the Caribbean island of Jamaica, or Jamaica in the New York borough of Queens. William Blue had worked in England as a sometime labourer and a chocolatier, and was transported to Botany Bay in 1796 at age twenty-nine, aboard the *Minorca*, for stealing sugar. All accounts paint Billy Blue (as he became known) as a spirited, canny character. He occupied a curiously respected position in white society, settling around The Rocks in Sydney with his English-born ex-convict wife and their six children. Governor Macquarie appointed him a harbour watchman and constable. He started a ferry service, which the governor used, and he amassed land. Paintings portray Billy Blue standing proud-eccentric, in the royal blue top hat or the naval jacket of which he was fond.

Black Jack Anderson is Australia's only known pirate. Wide accounts concur the African-American was as charismatic as he was ruthless. He arrived on the west coast of Australia in 1826, on the whaling vessel *Vigilant*. A brawl saw him accused of murder, and he took up residence with some of his crew in the dangerous waters of the Archipelago of the Recherche, on what is known as Middle Island. Under Anderson's command, the outlaws raided ships travelling between Adelaide and Albany. Anderson's body is rumoured to be buried on Middle Island. There are tales – shameful ones – of his brutalisation of local Kaurna people.

There are others, too many here to count. William Cuffay: a tailor by trade, and the son of a freed St Kitts slave, was transported from England in 1848 for his political action among the working classes. Orator and newspaper vendor Daniel Henderson, born in Kingston, Jamaica, is thought to have migrated to Australia voluntarily in 1865. These African-diaspora settlers display all the flair, ferocity, faults and foibles of their Anglo-Australian counterparts, yet they are largely absent from the knowledge of a vast number of Australians.

The seed for *Growing Up African in Australia* was born of a Twitter discussion between the editor and co-curators, noting the link between apartheid in South Africa and the genocide, dispossession and dehumanisation of First Nations people in Australia, through South Africa's modelling of apartheid on Queensland's *Aboriginal Protection Act* (1897). *These stories make me think it's high time we did a* Growing Up African in Australia *book*, this editor mused. Eighteen months later, amid allegations of rampant 'African gang crime' in Melbourne, and the Australian media's increasing demonisation of the African-Australian community, Magan Magan and Ahmed Yussuf contacted me and said: 'Remember your suggestion? It's now time.' We approached

Black Inc., who had already published the groundbreaking anthologies *Growing Up Asian in Australia* and *Growing Up Aboriginal in Australia*. The publishers took us on board.

Our first discussions regarding the collection were about scope. From the sixteenth to the nineteenth century, more than 10 million Africans, mostly from Central and West Africa, were dispersed across the Americas as human cargo in the transatlantic slave trade. They were sold to work on slave plantations, and as domestic servants, field workers or labourers. Australia has not been untouched by this 400-year trade in black lives. Recently, the work of academic Clinton Fernandes has confirmed that the proceeds of British slavery, and the financial compensation paid to slave-owners on abolition, helped establish significant and revered members of early colonial society in Australia.

Pointedly, we decided that *Growing Up African in Australia* would be an African-diaspora anthology that acknowledged this colonial truth, sharing stories from Australians of African descent, no matter the route their journey to Australia had taken. We called for submissions by Australians from across the African diaspora – from those who journeyed to Australia directly from the African continent to those who journeyed to Australia over hundreds of years and several generations via the United States, South America, the United Kingdom, the Caribbean or elsewhere.

This anthology was initiated, written, curated, edited and driven by members of the African-diaspora community in Australia. The process of compiling its contents has been nothing short of extraordinary. Reading every submission was life-affirming, and it was a genuine privilege for the curatorial team to read and consider passionate, engaging, innovative and heartfelt work from almost every region of the African diaspora. Our voices are strong, our roots run deep, and our stories are powerfully diverse.

We have grown up on potato farms in country Western Australia, in suburban rentals across New South Wales and in housing commission homes in the valleys of Tasmania. We hail from many different countries, including Somalia, South Sudan, Zambia, Jamaica, Brazil, Ghana, South Africa, Sudan, Zimbabwe, Kenya, Guyana and Egypt. We have been involved in landmark legal cases against the police forces sworn to protect us, become well-known reggae musicians on the Australian music scene, and started our own black dance companies. We have fled from war and poverty, and we have sought education and chased destinies. We have starred in popular children's television shows, become the head girl at our school, and endured bullying, isolation and discrimination. Our families are separated and strong; volatile and loving. Our lives and stories are just as ordinary, extraordinary, joyous and devastating as those of any other group of Australians, and they deserve to be written into Australian letters.

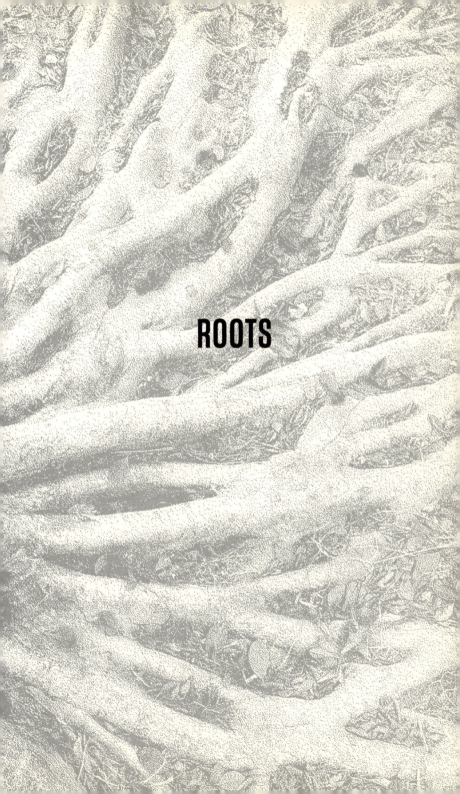

ROOTS

Potato Country

Kirsty Marillier

When we first moved to Australia, we lived in a small country town in the deep south of Western Australia. It was potato country. Everyone there, from memory, was a potato farmer or was somehow related to the region's famous potato-farming family, the Bendottis. They owned almost all of the land in the area. We lived on a Bendotti farm, and ate Bendotti potatoes straight out of the ground.

My family and I had immigrated to Australia six months prior, to Perth. My dad, a South African coloured man and a maths teacher, struggled to find work. It wasn't as if he was lacking in qualifications or experience, and Australia was in desperate need for good teachers in its schools. Nonetheless, he struggled.

A shy and intelligent man, noted for his shortness in stature but also for a level of endurance that inspires me to this day, Dad hunted ferociously for what felt like months and months for full-time work. My parents kept us going with the little bit of savings they had collected, while instilling hope in us every day that they had made the right decision and that Australian citizenship was on the horizon.

Then one Sunday afternoon, after many prayers and hopeful applications, Dad was offered a position at a school in Pemberton, in the south-west of Western Australia.

This development wasn't ideal. Life had taken a turn and we were now moving four hours south. In South Africa, Dad had had to work two jobs in order to get us to Australia: teaching during the day and delivering pizzas in our shitty bomb of a Toyota at night. He'd work long hours and come home late, and in the lead-up to catching that plane we never really saw him. It took my parents a long time to save up the money to get us here – an arduous time full of doubt and fear. So, they weren't exactly prepared to settle for anything less than the idyllic life they had hoped for: *Perth*.

For my struggling coloured parents, Perth was the mecca of the Western world, a place known for its sunshine, job opportunities and cheap housing estates. It was a paradise in which to start over and raise two young girls, away from rape, crime and apartheid. 'I'm telling you. You must come over to Australia, man! They are in need of teachers here!' friends told them. 'It's much safer. I can walk to the shops at night!'

When we were in South Africa, there were weekly sagas on the phone, where Aunty Connie would try to convince Mum that Perth was the utopia she had always been waiting for. 'We have a glass splashback in our kitchen. We live like kings, man!' she'd say. 'We even have spare dosh to go to the casino on weekends!'

....

Pemberton was tiny and quaint, renowned for its natural wonders in the surrounding forests. There was this massive dam full of trout, and a giant tree, which people were really proud of – I guess because it was the second-largest in the world. I wasn't entertained by these things.

The house we lived in was an old fibro shack on the Bendotti property. It had large windows and was surrounded by rolling hills and endless, grey sky.

We were in the middle of nowhere. As children, my sister and I had no idea why we were there. We had no understanding of the financial hardships our parents were going through, no knowledge of the challenge they were experiencing as they assimilated into a white-faced education system, no sense of the big grief they were feeling without culture and community. Mum's friends told her, 'Migrating to a new country is like the feelings one has during death.'

One of the things etched into my memory about that time was that it was always raining; it was always stupidly cold. For a group of Africans, this was a version of hell. And honestly, over the years, I've seen that whole part of my life as grey. From the colour of the sky to the colour of the potatoes to the colour of my mum's tears. All. Fucking. Grey.

We felt like we were trapped – in this new country, in this house and, unfortunately, with one another. Outside: vegetables and deep hills and wet earth. Inside: my parents, young, homesick and scared. Mum buried herself in cooking and crying; Dad hid away in the back room, always invested in his work. Displacement is seeing your mother cry in church while she sang hymns, while she opened the gate, after she got chased by cows, while steam danced on the windows, when she baked, when she cooked.

I remember looking at her once, her hair tucked into a stocking cap and her head buried in a tea towel, steam overflowing from her pots. She was cooking mince curry and listening to Brenda Fassie's 'Vul'indlela', like she would on most Sunday afternoons. She looked at me; I'd never seen her face soaked with so much sadness. I still haven't. Mum quickly shifted her expression to tough and assertive, a look that said: 'Don't worry, my child. I'll be fine.' Coloured women can be very stoic at times. It's something I admire deeply about them.

At first it was lovely eating food that had been grown and given to us. I guess it reminded me of Africa – eating freshly boiled amadumbes, butter melting off them and onto an old newspaper. But after a while, it got old. Mum tried to think of elaborate ways to cook each new batch of potatoes she'd receive: potato pie, potato curry, potato stew, *potato fucking kill me*.

As we started to understand the isolation and, I suppose, our incapacity to handle it, my sister and I became more and more inventive with our time, and our choice of games became curious and wild.

I'd pretend to be an old coloured woman living in a house. My sister would be a policeman. The officer would knock on the door of the woman's house, demanding she leave immediately because she was living in a house that had previously been owned by white people. I, the old woman, would fight the policeman with boxing gloves and yell, 'Fuck the apartheid!' over and over again, until he had a black eye and a limp and was gone. Mum gave me a hiding for saying *fuck*. She obviously couldn't see the integrity in my work.

We'd imagine what life would be like back home. We'd pretend to be on African soap operas. We'd have Kwaito rap battles and make dance videos to Earth, Wind & Fire. We'd dig up potatoes ourselves, and pick plums from high in the trees.

Those years were incredibly informative of who I was to become, as a woman of colour. It was when I first realised we were different, and that people may not have liked us because of that. We were the only brown family in an all-white town, and that felt strange. In South Africa, for all its problems, for all its hardships and lack of opportunity, we were never the only brown people in the room. Here, people looked at us with curiosity – sometimes curiosity laced with fear – and my parents were always spoken to with an element of distrust. Even as a kid, I could feel that. Perhaps it was for that reason we created our own worlds and stages and universes, maybe as a means of survival, for our parents and for ourselves.

Looking back, I can acknowledge how important that time was for my family and me, how my sister and I were two brown kids, suspended between place and culture, with nothing to do except to dig deeper within our imaginations and ourselves. Trying to create our own version of Africa within that small fibro house. It felt like the biggest and the smallest place in the world.

Sometimes, I wonder what things would be like if I could go back and reconcile myself with that time and place, with the cold and the starch. And I think about what I would tell those girls. Maybe I'd tell them to never stop doing what they're doing. Maybe I'd tell them to keep that fire in their hearts, to keep singing, keep dancing, keep taking up space, keep creating – to never stop creating a world that is exactly their own. I'd tell them to never stop being the wild, frizzy things that they are. I'd tell them that everything will be okay, and that one day, they're gonna be magic.

Power

Hope Mathumbu

The sharp sting on my thigh brings my mind back to the present, and I look up to see Mama's face glaring at me disapprovingly as Pastor Mnisi continues to scream into the microphone, beads of sweat trickling down his forehead. Naledi's smirking face pops out from behind Mama's shoulder, and she shakes her head at me in feigned disapproval. It's been two hours now, and it doesn't seem like we are any closer to the praise-and-worship part of the day. These visiting pastors always have to make a show of it, as though we have all the time in the world, like in Africa.

Jenny's birthday party started an hour ago, and Mama promised to drop me off in Collingwood to celebrate with her. I don't want to miss out on lunch because Jenny's mother is making hotpot and I don't know what that is. It doesn't matter to know – all the food that Jenny's mother makes is the best. Jenny thinks it's funny that I never had an Asian friend or Asian food before. Specifically, as she keeps telling me, a Vietnamese friend and Vietnamese food – because Asia is not a country, just as I keep telling her Africa isn't.

To be honest, this is also the first time I have had other African friends before, from countries that aren't right next door to my own. I never knew black people could be Muslim until I met all my North African friends. When I asked Papa about this over the phone, he struggled to explain it, and told me to make sure I keep going to church and pray for all my friends.

The phone card ran out of money before I could tell him I would.

Pastor Mnisi's voice has softened a bit now, and the band has started to play. Oliver is on the keyboard today, and my heart flutters with joy. I have never seen a man with relaxed hair before, almost to his shoulders. Each week he wears a perfectly ironed colour-coordinated suit with a matching tie, bowtie or handkerchief in his pocket. We have been going to this church for two years, and I have never seen him wear the same outfit. Today he is in purple, like the singer Prince. Naledi says he is gay, but I don't think so because he is always talking to women and laughing with them. Sometimes I see sesi Violet touching his hair and giving him advice, though God knows what she could possibly be telling him because she is always wearing the same old boring cornrow style, like me. Mama says it's too expensive to get our hair done the same way we did back home. Even though it's embarrassing, there are also not many black people in my day-to-day life to notice, and most of my black friends at school have their hair covered anyway, so I am some kind of novelty to people who don't know anything about how impoverished this two-month-old styling really looks. Sometimes I wonder if Mama is just punishing me and trying to keep me humble.

I don't understand how Oliver can have such perfect hair and clothes, and we have nothing. If my friends from home could see us now, they would be shocked. If Papa could see me now, too. Saying goodbye to him was the hardest thing I have ever done. It's only the second time I have seen him cry like a baby: shoulders shaking, and the pain rising out of his throat in uncontrollable wails. The first time I saw Papa cry was when my brother, Tinyiko, died – his only son. When he cried for us like that at the airport I knew I was loved. I knew it didn't matter that people pitied him for losing the continuation of his bloodline.

I promised myself that I would never get married, but find a way to have a boy-child that could continue the name. Zalabantu! If what sesi Violet tells us in youth Bible study is true, God probably won't like this plan to continue the bloodline. Auntie Grace has two children out of wedlock to different fathers and she still comes to church like there is nothing wrong. Mama sometimes offers them a lift home from church, but never goes inside the house like when she offers other people lifts.

I once asked Mama if I could make extra money babysitting Auntie Grace's kids now that I am fourteen years and nine months old. She smacked me across the head and told me that I am too young to know anything about looking after babies and that Auntie Grace's house isn't the best place to learn, either. I asked Naledi why Mama was so weird with Auntie Grace, and she just laughed and told me to mind my own business. I told her that nobody at church ever minds their own business, and she laughed again and said that's why they are all doomed. I have to remember to tell Dad about that.

The band is in full swing now, singing my favourite song: 'There Is Power in the Blood'. To Mama's joyful surprise, I stand up and lift my hands to the sky, singing along. I catch Naledi's disgusted eye and start to shake myself up and down to the tempo, singing, 'Lord send the power! Lord send the power!' I feel ashamed of myself for thinking that the only power I need is to survive this final hour so I can get to Jenny's birthday. The muscles in my stomach grind in unrelenting hunger, and I shake myself harder to the music.

Pastor Mnisi's voice booms through the microphone: 'Yes, send us the power, oh Lord, the power to transform ourselves through your sacred blood. The power to claim everlasting victory on this earth in your holy name. Yes, Lord, send the power!'

A lot of things changed when I got my blood, and none of them involved more power or victory. In fact, Mama told me that I wasn't allowed to play sport anymore because of my blood, so I joined the debating team. I am surprisingly good at it so far.

The beat quickens, and I feel the blood rush to my head as I scream to the Lord for more power. The bass from the music reaches from my toes, and spreads right up my body and through my chest as I jump up and down in pure manic joy. I am so caught up in the celebration that I fail to notice the gradual dimming of my surroundings, as my body shuts down and drops to the floor.

'Sagwadi, Sagwadi?!' Sharp stings across my cheeks bring my mind back to the present, and my eyes open to see Mama's scared face looking down at me. Pastor Mnisi's triumphant face pops out from behind her shoulder, nodding in approval. 'It's okay, Mama, she is fine. The Holy Spirit has moved her today.' He kneels beside me and reaches his clammy hand forward onto my forehead, and I am overwhelmed by the sour smell of sweat and Old Spice. I close my eyes and think of my own father, who wears Old Spice, but doesn't sweat as much. I surrender to the cacophony of voices in prayer around me, as I am baptised by the occasional spittle from Pastor Mnisi as he speaks in tongues. I am grateful for the noise, as I feel my stomach twisting in agonising hunger. While I am here, I may as well whisper a prayer of my own.

God never answers my prayers the way I need them answered. After the service, people flock to Mama to compliment her out-fit, and her God-fearing daughters. Naledi is obviously irritated at all the fuss, because she wishes she could have been the star of the show today. Sesi Violet invites Mama to lunch at her house and mentions that Pastor Mnisi will be attending before flying home later in the evening. Mama accepts the invitation and says we will all go to Frankston to sesi Violet's house.

I realise that not only have I missed Jenny's birthday, but I have also missed tonight's episodes of *Big Brother* and *Charmed*, because Frankston is on the other side of the world. As we walk to the car, I try to softly whisper to Mama that she promised to take me to Jenny's birthday, but she pretends not to hear me. As we are about to drive off, Oliver rushes to the car and asks for a lift to sesi Violet's house, where he too has been invited to lunch. I thank God for his small mercies as Oliver slides into the backseat beside me, smelling sweeter than any other man I have ever met. I catch Naledi's eye in the rear-view mirror as I try to hide my smile.

Her Mother's Daughter

Nyadol Nyuon

My daughter's daughter, you have come? She stretched to her toes and reached out to kiss my cheek, but she could only manage to reach my neck – I was too tall, no longer the child she once held in her arms.

It had been more than twenty years since I had seen my grandmother. I was now returning with my mother to see her. I knew she was getting old and I wanted to see her at least one more time before she passed away. She was my only grandparent still alive. The shameless indifference of war means that families become strangers. War reduces the most intimate relationships to meaningless connections. For me, the war not only separated me from my grandmother; I was also separated from my mother and knew little of my father. I grew up with fragments of who they are, the broken links of kinships.

I was too young to even remember the year I was separated from my mother. It was sometime in the early 1990s. It was not until my father was killed in 1996 that I saw her again. On the day we reunited, she was dressed in black. The dark, voluminous hair I remembered was clipped to the skull. She was very thin, her eyes so deeply sunken into the sockets they looked like mere black holes. When she saw me, she dropped to her knees and cried. I stood there stiffly, like a tree trunk. It did not occur to me that tears were appropriate for the occasion.

As for my father, he was killed before I knew much of him.

My father was absent for most of my life. I saw him occasionally when he visited our home in Kenya, and even then, he was busy in meetings. Dad was a freedom fighter: a high-ranking commander in the guerrilla movement waging a war for an independent state – South Sudan. He was so committed to this cause that my only memories of my father are attached to his struggle for liberation. I have no recollection of a shared private moment between us. I have some memories of talking to him, but sometimes I am not sure whether these are the desperate inventions of my mind – a need to hold on to something of a man who should have been a part of my life.

The only real stories I know of my father are those told to me by others. Most of these I have heard because people have stopped me randomly on the streets in Kenya, saying that I look like my father. They tell me he was a brave, intelligent man. They praise his wit, and his courage to have given his life for his country; they tell me I should be proud to be his daughter. I generally leave these interactions with a clear sense of what my father meant to some people and even maybe to his country, but what remains unclear is what he left for his family. In some ways, he had no choice. For my father, my mother, my grandmother and me, war made the choices for us, and made the distance and separation normal.

Growing up without my mother and father left me with few memories of love – what it looked and felt like. The little sense of love I had was a single memory of my grandmother. In those lonely times as a young child, I would imagine nestling into her and then waking up to a warm cup of fresh cow's milk. I still remember the scent – it was like butter on fire.

On the day I met my grandmother again, for a moment, the years and the distance did not seem to matter. She was so happy to see me and my mum return that she began to dance and sing, performing circular movements around her little compound. She would stop, return to my side and hug me, and then go back to dancing and singing again. The neighbours began to pour into my grandmother's compound, and we were surrounded by a group of curious children.

As we interacted with everyone, it became clear to me that my grandmother was considered the leader of the small town. She had the community telephone in her home, and people consulted her on the progress of a number of things. I was told that she was the first person to have built a house here, nearly two hours' walk from the main town, Gambella, and that all these homes had sprung up around her. Everyone, even the children, knew her name – Man Mary, meaning Mary's mother. I asked her why she had chosen to come and live out here, without running water or much security. I told her we could afford to house her in the town and employ someone to look after her. She tilted her head to look at me and, with a smile, she said, 'People in the towns are lazy, they do not work or farm. Out here, I can work. If I do not work, I will die. Come look at my farm.'

As we walked around, my grandmother pointed out the boundaries of her farm. All over were green plantations of maize. On our way back to her compound, she showed me three partially completed buildings. She said she was building them in case any of her children chose to return – she wanted them to have a home ready. For my grandmother, home was here; all her descendants were to come back to these ancestral lands.

When we got to the compound, it was about time to leave. My grandmother organised for the women who were around to sing some gospel songs. Then we prayed. My grandmother was very religious, and she raised my mother with the same beliefs.

I would see that faith comfort my mother when nothing else could. She often told me, 'My God is my husband, my friend and my psychology.' By psychology, she meant her God was her counsellor when she felt overwhelmed.

After the prayers, my grandmother escorted us back to the road. We reached a crossroad, with one of the roads branching off towards Itang, the town where I was born. My grandmother mentioned that she was intending to walk to Itang to ask that one of her cows be brought back. She wanted to sacrifice it, to thank God for my return. We hugged, and she walked off towards Itang, Mum and I waiting at the side of the main road. We flagged down a number of cars and lorries, hoping that one would stop to take us back to Gambella.

Growing up, I had often wondered where some of my characteristics had come from. I could not explain why I did things the way I did or why I felt as I did. I often felt like a stranger to myself. Watching my grandmother on the day we met again, I saw some of who I am in her. I went to bed that night feeling reconciled with part of myself.

In many ways, what I had seen in my grandmother I had seen before in my mother. For a long time I did not want to admit this because of the anger I had towards her. This anger stemmed from trying and failing to forge a life together as a family, as a mother and a daughter, after so many years apart. After so many years without a mother, I just wanted someone to look after me – not someone who came with her own load in life, a load that required understanding, which I was too immature to have, and sometimes too selfish to give.

It would not be until I had a child of my own that I would realise that mothers are not just mothers; they remain their own persons, with their own dreams and aspirations, which do not have to derive from their identity as care-givers. I would realise that my bond with my mother was complicated by culture, and made extraordinarily difficult by war. I would understand that my mother stood as the total sum of what had happened to her – much of which she could not control – and that, in many ways, she had survived with as much dignity as one could wrangle out of such a situation. I would learn that when she spoke to me, she was sometimes speaking to things I could not see, and would never fully comprehend. I would learn all this in Australia, because the chance to live in safety allowed us to spend uninterrupted time together. It allowed us the luxury to not merely survive but to live in the full complexity of being a human being, instead of just a refugee.

Before we returned to Australia, my mother and I travelled through Ethiopia, where my grandmother lived, and to South Sudan. I saw her treated with a level of honour that I had never seen before. She was respected, she was known, and she was relied upon for advice and counsel. She had a voice – a strong voice. It was so strong that her people had once picked her to represent them as a member of parliament.

I could not help but compare that to her life in Melbourne, where she struggled to find work as a cleaner or an aged-care worker. I had watched her struggle with the language, struggle to understand the complex letters sent by Centrelink, insurance companies or banks. It is a blunt contrast to go from having a voice strong and clear enough for the national parliament of South Sudan to struggling on a phone call, nearly in tears, in Australia. It was as if her tongue had been cut out, as if she was socially crippled in this society.

Many people assume that everyone wants to come to Australia. I have wondered whether my mother ever wanted to.

Mum, like many parents, came to this country for her children. She wanted my siblings and me to have a better life, or at least a chance to try to make something of ourselves. No matter how bad her country was, she was industrious enough to have survived – maybe even thrived. I had seen her create magic from little. She ran a small business in the Kakuma refugee camp, in northern Kenya. She negotiated for land to build our home in an area denied to refugees for a long time. We never went a single day without food in Kakuma, when many struggled.

I have always felt that my mother would have stayed in Africa were it not for us. I knew this after our trip to Africa, because she glowed when we were there. She seemed more alive. That light appears to diminish each day she stays in Australia. In coming to Australia, my mother made a sacrifice necessitated by war, and by love – a love for her children.

I cannot escape the fact that I was a big reason for that sacrifice: as her own light grew weak, mine was made brighter by immigrating to Australia.

We came to Australia from a refugee camp that had no running water or electricity and barely met our basic needs for survival. My family depended on food rations distributed fortnightly by the United Nations.

At the time, I attended Kakuma Secondary College, one of three secondary schools servicing the refugee camp of nearly 90,000 people. In choking heat, I sat in a class of about sixty to eighty students. On each bench, around four students sat together on desks that stretched less than an arm's length. I was approaching the end of my secondary schooling and was desperate to leave the camp. There was no university in Kakuma, and my mother could not afford to pay for further education outside the camp.

It had been a couple of years since we had submitted our

application for resettlement to Australia. We had heard nothing. My mother would sing gospel songs and pray each night, pleading with God that our application be approved. Sometimes I sang along with her, but most of the time I listened silently, waiting for my turn to persuade God on the 'wisdom' of letting my family and me resettle in Australia.

When Mum stopped singing, I would take over. I waited until my mother had finished singing and praying because I thought God would be in a better mood. When all was quiet, so quiet that I could clearly hear my thoughts, I would begin negotiating with God. I pleaded and promised that if my family made it to Australia, and I got a university education, I would be a good Christian; I would always be grateful, never complain and always, always listen to my mother.

The day our approval for resettlement arrived was the most joyous of my life. On the night before our travel to Australia, I tried to memorise the numbers on our tickets – all ten of them. I was afraid they would get lost and we would not be allowed on the plane. I was not taking any chances. On the day of our departure I remember being very angry at my mother: she was taking too long to say goodbye, and I was afraid we would miss the plane and our chance for a better life.

We arrived in Melbourne on the night of 15 March. As the plane descended towards Melbourne, I thought the world has been literally turned upside down. It was dark above, but below was a magnificent display of lights that twinkled like a million stars. I could not contain my excitement. For my mother, this journey across oceans to the unknown might have been a sacrifice. For me it was a chance of a new home.

Little did I know then that soon enough doubts would creep in: Could someone who looked like me call this home? Was home something you embraced, or did it also have to embrace you back? Would I always be seen as a conditional citizen, to whom citizenship was not a right, but a gift that could only be kept by an impeccable character? Would any mistakes – even mistakes made or wrongs committed by people who looked like me – mean that my stay in this new home became no longer acceptable? Would any complaint, any sign of ungratefulness, be deemed a lack of appreciation of the opportunities presented to me? Should I consider a backup plan – go back where I came from? Where was home?

I was born in Ethiopia, to parents of South Sudanese background, and I grew up in Kenya. When I moved to Australia, I had never been to South Sudan; in fact, South Sudan did not exist as a state at the time. Where is home? I have never really felt like I belong in any of those countries.

However, even in my confusion, I felt I was better placed than my siblings. Arriving here even younger than me, several have known only this life, but many will see only their blackness – a marker that they do not belong here. I wonder what it would feel like to feel Australian but happen to be black, to wake up one day into the knowledge of your blackness and what that means to some people. How do you hold on to a sense of belonging when it is so often assaulted by racism?

All of these questions were yet to occur to me, on 15 March, when I stepped into the bright lights of Tullamarine airport, and walked into a new life.

Blending Families

Shona Kambarami

Ben is racist. That's not unusual – lots of people are. In fact, globally, racists are having a bit of a moment. I first became conscious to racism at eight years old. I wanted to be a gymnast then. I'd been looking forward to the final session of gymnastics training all week because after watching all my teammates win 'gymnast of the week', I knew it was my turn (*everyone will win an award by the end of the year*). Showing off, I spent most of the session teaching Ana how to do a handstand. I was gutted when I lost the final award of the year to her (*for her amazing handstands*). She was the only one among us to win twice. I looked around, and for the first time I realised everyone else was white, including Coach Norris. It wasn't that he didn't see me; it was that he did.

I never went back to gymnastics. Like I said, lots of people are racist.

Ben's racism even makes a convoluted sort of sense: he lives in a predominantly white town, in a predominantly white state, in a predominantly white, colonised Australia. He doesn't really know anyone who isn't white, either. The problem, of course, is that Ben now knows *me*, and I'm not white. And while under different circumstances he might be able to avoid spending time with me, maintaining the monochromy of the people in his life, that's not possible anymore. You see, I'm in love with Ben's son.

I've loved white men before. My first crush was Josh, the teenage son of my kindy teacher, whom I only saw twice, but loved with the singularity of focus that only a child has. I was going to be the first Black princess in the British Royal Family, well before Meghan Markle (*if Harry could just meet me, he'd know we were meant to be*); I pledged allegiance to Nick Carter in the heyday of the Backstreet Boys. In my defence, there weren't very many Black people on television or in fairytales for me to fall in love with back then; Prince Charming was always white.

Celebrity romance dreams foiled, I happened to be single when, about four years ago, I met a wonderful man. We connected in the most millennial way: it was during the rise of the dating app (*everyone is doing it*) and attractiveness was the most valuable currency in the love economy. One swipe right, an hour of awkward texting, a five-minute phone call, a wonderful four-hour conversation over red wine and overpriced pizza, and a romantic night (*I usually don't do this on the first date*) later, we were in it. It took us a little bit longer than that evening to know this, but we fell in love that first day, and it has been as extraordinary a love story as any ever told.

We know that our relationship is political, whether we want it to be or not. When we walk into cafés in our little part of Australia for our weekend ritual of eggs Benedict and coffee (*soy latte for me, double espresso for him*), heads turn, conversations falter and whispers punctuate the embarrassing silence. In every neighbourhood, we count the number of interracial couples we meet, and get excited when they are the same combination as us (*do you think it'd be weird if we high five them as we walk by?*).

My family is *African* Black, which is different from non-African Black. If the years of having them not acknowledge my ex-boyfriend (*he's not African! He didn't go to uni!*) were anything to go by, this relationship would be in for a rough time. But it wasn't. Apparently, history teaches us lessons – ones even African parents are sometimes willing to learn. My family was not going to risk alienating me by insulting another of my partners; lemons to lemonade, as they say.

Him's family, Jewish and un-diverse, had never had to negotiate an interracial relationship before. Or so I thought. In retrospect, his prevarication should have been a sign.

It took Ben almost two and a half years to meet me. In many ways, the interaction was forced: his daughter announced her engagement, and everyone agreed that a first meeting at the wedding was a bad idea. By then, Him had been introduced, in a trial-by-fire kind of way, to my people. A year and a half earlier it had also taken a wedding – my cousin's – for my family to meet, and fall in love with, him. We hadn't prepared at all for that first meeting. I'd invited him to the wedding in the shower one morning (*hey, my cousin's getting married in Cape Town in six months, wanna come?*) and he'd agreed without a thought. We didn't discuss what his turning up as my date would communicate to my family, and after four days of a marriage inquisition (*in our culture, if you're meeting the family, you're announcing your engagement. So, when is it?*) the naivety of our young relationship was exposed. Families take introductions seriously. We vowed to do better next time.

So, six weeks before Ben celebrated his daughter and her fiancé's love under the chuppah, he pretended to celebrate ours. Ben was uncomfortable, but trying hard to overcome it – he smiled widely, and often, and took almost every opportunity to ask me about the weather (*so is it really unbearably hot in Africa?*). The awkwardness spanned the weekend: I tried to hug him when we met but was rebuffed (*I don't like hugs, sorry*). He walked into the kitchen at 5.00 am in his underwear and was too polite to leave without saying good morning, and I was too stunned to answer, so we stood there, Ben, near-naked, and me, wide-eyed. His welcome speech before Shabbat dinner included a recitation of the history of the Zimbabwean people and a memorised greeting in 'African' (*sawubona! Did I get it right?*). Even though 'African' isn't a language, and we don't speak Zulu in Zimbabwe, I appreciated the effort. The meeting went well.

Six weeks later, at The Wedding™, our interactions were diluted. The house was a thoroughfare for the busybody aunties, party-planning sisters and cousins, babies and excited well-wishers that populate any family wedding. Ben was more animated than ever. I was welcomed, and felt as much a part of the family as anyone else, until his speech at the reception (*when a son gets married, it is the continuation of the family name; when a daughter gets married, it's the continuation of the Jewish people*) revealed to me why he would never quite accept me. In the fog of celebration, I shrugged it off.

After, for a time, I was included in the pre-Shabbat family emails, and it seemed that I was in. So when Ben got sick, I suggested that we go and visit to find out how he was. Him's ambivalence was unusual. For weeks, I pushed (*any more news about your dad? Should we go visit?*) and Him resisted, until one day, I wished I hadn't. It had been a month or so since Ben's emails had stopped coming, and a month since his illness had worsened. I made that connection after that night – the night Him told me that Ben had asked for me, specifically, not to come (*I don't want her here*).

There was no explanation from Ben, which made it harder to mould the nature of my outrage. Was it my Blackness? My non-Jewishness? Was it my personality? My job? My African-ness?

Did I say something? Do something? When? Where? How? The absence of logic to this psychic violence was even more infuriating than the action.

Perhaps that's part of the insidiousness of racism. There is no reason that justifies it. Nothing Ben could have said would have made me better understand his objection to my personhood. It is senseless, and derives its power from that senselessness. After a lifetime of living in this skin, and the consequences of the rage it incites in people without it, I have learnt this: there is nothing I can do to make myself acceptable to Ben. I did nothing to deserve his scorn other than to exist, and to fall in love with his son, sins for which I am unwilling to repent.

Perhaps the missing link here, the question you may be asking, is *so how do you know it's racism?* Well, there is no real answer for that. How do you prove a bias that someone is unwilling to acknowledge? Ben would never admit to being racist, perhaps because he really believes he isn't. In his conversations with his son, he denies it as a motivating factor for his objections to our relationship – no, he's more concerned about culture, about family, about religion; never mind that I could embrace the culture, I *am* family, and I could convert to the religion. Racism, it seems, is never about race, even when it is.

I want to confront Ben. I want to sit with him, share a meal and make him listen while I tell of the undeserved shame and humiliation his actions have caused me. I want to see Ben justify his cruelty when faced with my tears. I want him to stop seeing me as what I am not and start seeing me as what I am: a woman who loves his son, and wants to love *him*, even now. And if I'm honest, if nothing else is achieved by such a confrontation, the act of standing up for myself in the face of racism is reward enough. In generations past, I would never have been afforded the opportunity, and so, in a small way, it would feel like progress.

But my father-in-law, Ben, is sick. As he is faced with his mortality, my confronting his racism might be more of an injury to the family than his being racist in the first place. Perhaps his illness both motivates his renewed boldness and shields him from the consequences.

This is what it feels like. Somehow, my love for Him and my compassion for Ben compel me to be silent. But the silence feels like a violence of its own. The silence feels like Ben's licence to do me harm, like a devolution, a betrayal of self; like a loss.

The Whitest White Girl

Prue Axam

I was the whitest white girl ever. I grew up in the north-west of Sydney, in Eastwood. My family has been there for hundreds of years. After that we lived in Cheltenham, which is near Beecroft. I went to the same primary school my father went to. I went to primary school with the kids of people my parents had gone to primary school with. It was a very local experience. There was not a lot of diversity of any kind – or, at least, I didn't feel there was. I was a curious kid, so I did find that a little boring.

I started kindergarten in 1983. That was around the time that was leading up to the celebration of the bicentenary. A lot of families got swept up in family history and genealogy. My mum became quite passionate about it, even though she was from England, and began researching my dad's side of the family. She worked with my grandfather on it as well. He hadn't finished primary school, so he struggled a bit with the documents. He was a typically patriarchal Australian man but he was very loved by his family.

My mother found out that we were descended from a lot of convicts, on many different transportations. The first Axams, the surname that I have, came to Australia in 1830, but we'd also descended from a lot of convicts before them. She finally got to the First Fleet, which was the gold of family genealogy at that time. That's when she found out about John Martin and John Randall, the two men of African descent from whom I'm descended, who arrived here on the First Fleet.

She was very excited, but she was hesitant to tell my grandfather. When she told him, he was a bit shocked. She told my dad, and my brother and me, and we were really excited. My grandfather took a bit of persuading. His own grandmother, Emily, had apparently been very conscious of her darker skin colour. She'd worn long sleeves and gloves all the time. The family thought she might have been part Aboriginal. That would have been the more reasonable explanation than being related to African-American former slaves who'd ended up in England, and were then transported to Australia.

In honesty, I think that my little world was so white that I didn't really understand what that information meant to our family. I remember asking what a slave was, because I didn't know. I certainly knew nothing of the history of America. What I knew was the story of the bicentenary and the First Fleet as it was being told in schools at the time. It was kind of made light of, how we were suddenly African, and how we were going to cope with the fact that we were now African. My brother loved the opportunity to support the then world-beating West Indies cricket team.

I did have an interest in history. Not so much the early colony as such, because we were force-fed this jolly version of it in primary school and I was a bit tired of it all. I would sometimes use this story, about having black ancestors who arrived on the First Fleet, in that breaking-the-ice game where you have to say two things about you that are true, and one thing about you that is untrue, and the other people have to guess which is the untrue thing.

It's a long time ago that these black ancestors of mine lived, but it's also not. For me, it's seven generations ago. The way my mother got me to understand it all was by explaining that my grandfather's grandmother, Emily, was the great-granddaughter of one of the men who arrived on the First Fleet. My ancestors had very long lifespans – they lived for longer than was typical of that time. Emily died only a few months before I was born, so I didn't know her, but it feels close.

My mother explored this all deeply. This was before the internet, so everything took longer. She used to go off to Sydney's Mitchell Library. There were two genealogy societies there. I used to go with her, because I was into history and I liked looking at all the records. I was a nerd – a handy little nerd. Because there was a lot of excitement about family histories at the time, families would share information they found with one another. These convict forebears of mine had rather large families, so there were a lot of people looking for information. John Martin had eleven children, and those children also went on to have quite large families. I read that there are estimated to be 20,000 descendants of John Martin, so there are a lot of people who have this same family history, but you sort of have to know it's possible to go and look for it or seek it out.

I do think this information has had a bearing on the way I think about some things. In the past few years, there's been a lot of conversation about Australia Day and the date it should be celebrated. I had a conversation at work last week with a woman who said, 'What's the point in changing the date? It won't fix anything.' I think we should at least consider an alternative date. It will make a difference to the people who are saying, 'It hurts us that Australia Day is celebrated on 26 January.' I also have ancestors who arrived on the First Fleet, and I don't think 26 January 1788 was the greatest day of their lives. I had never said that aloud, or even really thought deeply about that, until recently. I love this country, but it frustrates me as well.

I'm a contemplative person. I lived in America for a year, and I remember thinking, *Australia is such a blunt instrument of a country*. I would love Australian history to include some of these stories that are amazing and that we can grow and learn from. It's sort of my job in a way to carry the privilege of being the whitest white girl ever as lightly as I can. The lives that my black ancestors John Martin and John Randall had would have been terrifying. It's hard to even contemplate the things they would have encountered.

John Martin and John Randall were both from the north of the United States. Martin was working on boats, and Randall was a musician. I think they both answered the call of the British, who were saying if you come and fight for us (which meant them running away), then if we lose the war, we'll bring you to London and provide you with some kind of pension. They weren't really expecting to lose the war, but they did. Once they were in England, in order to claim the pension they had to be able to prove who they were. There was no way to prove that they'd been slaves, and that they'd fought in the war, so they were just left destitute. Both were convicted of theft for stealing food or clothes, and that's why they were sent to Australia. John Martin was given quite a light sentence. He served most of it in England, and by the time he got to Australia he only had a year to go. They only sent the conviction records with the Third Fleet, though, which meant the records didn't arrive in Sydney until 1792. He served two extra years when he should have been a free man.

The number of records that do exist is actually quite remarkable. The two men arrived in 1788, but by 1810 both John Martin and John Randall were living around the Pennant Hills area, near where I grew up. One of them was more 'successful' than the other. John Martin became the constable of his area, and by doing that he got extra provisions and was able to feed his family better. John Randall, I think, moved back to the city. In the subsequent generations, Martin's descendants were mostly still on small holdings around Pennant Hills. They did come here and prosper.

It's important to look to history, and to have the fullest sense of yourself that you can. I do think knowing this about my family has changed the way I think about things. My partner and daughter are mixed-race, so that means I also have much more awareness of race-related discussions than I had in the past. The world is a very big place.

Remember

Muma Doesa

Back when I was too young to fly the coop,
Just labelled as a minority group,
With my sisters, I was always in the loop
Warm embraces, laughter
Back then, things were harder.

I remember carrying a couch home from the shop,
Delivery cost a lot.
When the couch dropped
Dad said, 'Pick it up, don't stop.'
He was a teacher and gave many lectures
Taught us to stay strong when the world tests ya.

We used to argue, fire in our eyes,
He always taught us to hold our heads up high.
School during the day and work at night,
Too young to know how to improve my life.

One sister went to Africa, heart filled with hope
Eventually she was teaching people how to vote.
The election where Mandela came to power –

My thirteen-year-old eyes shed a tear that hour.
Victory poured down like a sun shower.

Meanwhile, back home I had my first swig of alcohol
Out my mouth my first smoke would blow
My curiosity never failed me,
Listened to Billie Holiday daily;
Inspired by the voices of jazz ladies
I always wished I could be that way.
Sister braided my hair at the start of the school day.
I used to catch hunger pain blues
Five-finger discounts were the rule
Don't judge a girl by her worn-out shoes.

People caught on to clues I was different from others,
Siblings were girls but taunted like brothers,
Always did my own thing, I never was smothered.
Didn't care what the neighbours thought, got it from
    my mother.
Didn't fall in line, couldn't be like others.
Deep down I knew I had bigger fish to fry,
When adventure called, I just had to reply!

Learnt our history verbally, not from a page,
Dad told me stories of when he was my age
Growing up as a young man in apartheid,
He loved music but his mission was to educate.
More knowledge in my head than food on my plate,

But looking back, I can't hate.

Forgiveness is the biggest step to heal the pain,

Love brought us back together again

So I tell our story with no shame.

THE PLAYGROUND

Winston

Lauren Mullings

Winston was always the loudest person on our street. The suburb I grew up in, Jordanville, was so innocuous that when one day they just took it off the map, no one even put up a fight.

Winston was also the loudest person in Jordanville, or Chadstone, as it became known. As if being a family of weird Jamaicans wasn't enough.

I used to cringe when I heard his voice booming down the street. 'Yo, yo, yo, yo, yo!'

The local kids would come racing down the road in their hypercolour t-shirts and happy pants, eager for his attention. 'Winston! Hey, baba! Baaa-baaa!' To them, he was nothing short of a celebrity.

To eight-year-old me, who wanted nothing more than to blend in, he was hugely embarrassing. By then I had experienced just about enough of 'sticking out' in my nearly all-white neighbourhood.

Winston had no plans to be the shy retiring type, not even for his kids. He was tall, black and present. Far from the conservative suit-wearing Jamaicans I had seen in our family photo album, my dad was part ragamuffin, part family man: a cutlass-carrying rudeboy with a bushman spirit.

He enjoyed being mortifyingly inappropriate and was often lewd, but *lawd* he was funny. His stories were pure theatre, full of pauses dragged out for effect, designed to draw in every member of his audience.

That audience most likely included one of his Jamaican friends, my mum, me, a kid from up the street and, say, the gasman. I would peer up from my Barbies and observe him mid-story, throwing his arms around wildly or giving imaginary measurements with his workman's hands.

When he thought his story had everyone on the edge of their seats, he would jump up and throw down a twist. As an insider, I knew all of his tricks, and that for his next one he would walk away at the height of the narrative drama. Like all good show-men, he would leave his audience shocked. This shock would quickly turn to delight as his crazyman laugh would ring through our concrete commission house.

Winston worked the night shift at a factory that made, among other things, toothpaste and Lucozade, crates of which could be found in our bathroom or stacked up messily in the kitchen. He hated his job, really, but figured money was better spent on backing me and my mum to keep at our schooling than on train-ing for his career. Mum had gone back to long-term study, and had her eye on getting into law at the local university. Winston wasn't an academic man, and he knew it. But he was razor sharp, and always able to read between the lines.

In the daytime, despite his miserable job, Winston would seem relaxed and happy. He'd listen to lovers rock, a style of reg-gae music, from our oversized sound system in the lounge, and whistle along unsuccessfully through the gap in his front teeth (which I'm told was the result of an accident with a cricket ball when he was a boy).

Mum was combining study with several jobs, including work-ing the checkout at Safeway. Winston would take me there to see her and show me how to shoplift, despite the obvious risks for my mother. 'Look pon the bloodclaat price a' cashews. Them try to thief me, but I thief them back!'

To make ends meet he'd sell a little weed, too – just within the legal limits, of course. He got caught once or twice, but when the police arrived he was so blasé that they let him keep one of his plants. 'And then,' he told me afterwards, his voice building in a triumphant crescendo, 'they sat down to smoke with me!'

Sometimes he would stalk the house for hours in the middle of the night, talking to himself. On certain days he might be worrying about money, or a handful of other things I wouldn't understand until I was much older. The furrow in his brow would tell us that something was up, but we just left him to his pacing. On occasion, I would overhear him having conversations with his dead relatives. Once, he told me his Aunt Lydia had come to him in a dream and told him there was something wrong with my unborn sister. Lydia Ann Rose was born some months later, cute as a button and with Down syndrome.

Inside our house, it was Jamaica. Strict and orderly. Chicken was bought only from one 'approved' butcher and seasoned a good twenty-four hours before cooking. Curfews and bedtimes were enforced. Children were seen and not heard during The Cricket. Tension was relieved through a good old-fashioned slagging match. We were all vocal, but only my parents stood a chance of winning an argument in our household.

Our spare room was regularly let out to fresh-off-the-boat Jamaicans. Though charitable, Winston was always eager to spend time with one of his own, and I suspect that was the true reason for his generosity. He would say he found someone 'down the road' and bring them home to live with us, much to my mum's frustration. The resulting stand-offs would go on for days, during which time I would leg it to neighbours across the road. There I enjoyed a second life, with a kind of surrogate family where everything seemed kind of liberal compared with the strict Mullings household. Kerry and Bert didn't screen flicks for 'adults only' content like my parents did. Kerry bought white bread and let me watch *Top Gun*.

Unlike the kids at my primary school, the kids across the street didn't seem to care that I was mixed-race, or that my dad was dark-skinned. They were too busy picking on one another and arming me with a colourful arsenal of cruel insults: 'Retard!', 'Poof!', 'Gaylord!' I savoured each one, writing all of them down in my diary for later use against the bigger kids in the playground who had inherited their parents' racist tendencies.

One day at school a quick-witted kid that I had naively thought was my friend realised he had made a social faux pas by hanging out with me, the black kid. He announced to everyone on the play equipment that he would now address me as 'Squishy'.

'That's your name now,' he explained to me, 'because of your ugly, squishy nose.' I cried all the way home and wrote the word in the back page of my diary, liquid papering it over immediately afterwards.

At my school, bullying seemed to be a sport. In the first weeks after I started there, I walked around with my head held high, like the Jamaican athletes – toned, black and muscular, with strides like panthers' – I had seen streaming to victory at the 1988 Olympics. Yet as the weeks wore on, the bullying wore me down. At dinner, our household sat in silence as Ben Johnson was stripped of his medal for cheating, and at school I continued to be bullied without intervention.

I asked my mum for advice on how to deal with bullying. 'One day you will look back and be glad you were different,' she said, clearly taken aback. 'Your dad says that you will always have to work harder than other kids to get the same things. Because you are black.'

'Brown,' I corrected her. 'Because I am *brown*.'

I knew she had told Winston about the conversation when he confronted me in the hallway the next day, clearly amused. 'Aww, hon. You brown now? Mmm-hmm. Your choice.'

During school holidays, I would stay in for hours enjoying a new hobby – looking for movies and television programs with black people in them. I'd look forward to the Sunday-afternoon movie matinee. Winston would raise his eyebrows but say nothing as mammies in headscarves flashed across the screen and I bobbed around in imitation like Shirley Temple – *tappy-tappy-tap*. 'Look, Dad. Our people!' I would say.

Still, the summer was good to me. I discovered that a Ugandan kid lived around the corner. His mum seemed delighted that we could play together, despite Winston jokingly calling him 'Idi Amin'.

But inevitably the holidays came to an end and it was back to school again, where things seemed to gather steam. Bigger kids would come over to pick on me in the schoolyard. The name-calling became more vicious. An 'ABC', I learnt, was an 'Aboriginal bum cleaner'. And apparently I was one, as I had come out of 'the wrong hole'.

I became anxious and withdrawn. My parents kept encouraging me to fight back, but these kids seemed so much bigger than me. When my class rival finally wrestled me to the ground and followed through with drop kicks to my face, Winston and my mother were summoned to the school.

The bully had anticipated the evident foot mark on my cheek being something of an issue, and quickly took control of the story, telling her parents I had called her a 'white bitch'. Although this was utterly nonsensical, I glanced over to see my parents looking out of their league, staring compliantly at their shoes, as if waiting for it all to be over. I was outraged. I expected as much from the school, but from Winston, my tall, proud-to-be-black dad?

There was no such thing as 'racist bullying' in 1980s Australia, so the principal resolved to remove us both from the school population, popping us in a room together to work out our differences.

I was furious. Why was no one coming to my rescue? This wasn't how it unfolded on *The Cosby Show*. Mr and Mrs Huxtable would have pulled their little darling out of there so fast the principal's head would be left spinning. If this were *Diff'rent Strokes*, Mr Drummond would have had Rudy and Arnold rehoused in no time!

Why was *I* being punished? I had watched the *Roots* telemovie just the month before, with Winston. He'd roared with laughter as Kunta Kinte took a whipping for insisting on giving his African name. 'Just tell him what your name is, Toby!' I couldn't understand how my parents were not afforded the privilege of fighting back.

Feeling let down, I started to deal with matters in my own way. I developed a strategy. Within Jamaican culture is a complicated set of rituals that, if practised every day, is said to provide immunity against harassment. I told some girls that performing these rituals would stop the boys in the playground from teasing them. Of course, those powers extended to protection from the boys and girls who were harassing me. This had a surprising effect – as my religion spread and our little group grew, I began to stand my ground.

Then one glorious day, the head bully came down with nits. The news spread like wildfire. What more proof could I offer that my voodoo powers were working?

A change was in the air. Rifts were breaking out everywhere. The kid with epilepsy was picked on by the fat kid; the fat kid was picked on by the girl who stomped on my face. Her parents' messy marriage was displayed for all to see: her dad would drag her mum back from her lover's house, while we kids would stare open-mouthed from the street.

A teacher tried to intervene in our playground wars with a trust exercise – we were supposed to confront all the other kids who had teased us. Seeing my chance, I made up wild, damning stories of which Winston would have been proud, parading around for dramatic effect, wagging my fingers at various suspects, condemning each and every kid who had picked on me and some who I suspected had thought about it. The group ate it up. Other kids followed suit with their own bogus stories. Letters were sent home. I was triumphant.

On telly, ABC was awash with weird new shows whose characters seemed to have mysterious ethnicities. Astroboy, Punky Brewster, Mysterious Cities of Gold. Punky Brewster had a black friend – her name was Cherry – and they would go to cool parties together where they would say 'no' to drugs. Run DMC and Milli Vanilli became the new staples on our big sound system. I bought a shell tracksuit and offered to decode the lyrics 'Informer' to anyone who would interested. After Viv Richards had popped by my house and Winston had cooked for him, I knew then I had school politics in the bag.

It wasn't long after that Winston moved out. Mum and I had noticed a change in his behaviour some time before – a kind of despondency, an unhappiness that seemed deep-rooted and incurable. He was dissatisfied. His stories, usually a wee bit elaborate, now seemed peppered with untruths. Had they always been?

It didn't matter. Now officially Little Miss Independent, I figured I didn't need him anyway. He'd show up unannounced to the house from time to time – when Mum graduated, for instance, and again when she finished her articles.

It was only many years later that I began to understand the complexities of Winston's life. The hero from my childhood, long discarded in my own fight to survive, came back to life as I shared stories with English friends about my childhood in Australia.

How could I have known that when Winston and I met he'd already lived many lifetimes? I knew little of how he'd migrated from his Jamaican homeland to new and sometimes hostile countries, of how he'd survived joblessness and brutish working conditions, of how he'd persisted through the daily racism and somehow thrived on the indifference toward him. He'd possibly overcompensated by having far too many wives and kids.

But somehow aware of the limits of his mortality, Winston had been training all of us – his tiny tribe of descendants – to stand on our own. And our collective refusal to follow convention may extend back further than any of us will ever know, far back into Winston's roots and beyond. His humour follows us, like a shadow, making light of any and every hardship and reminding us that it is our choice what things in life are serious.

Later, Winston moved out. Now officially Little Miss Independent, I figured I didn't need him anyway. He'd show up unannounced to the house from time to time – when Mum graduated, for instance, and again when she finished her articles.

I realise now that Winston had started training me to do things on my own. I just didn't realise it at the time.

Winston's refusal to follow convention was always part of me. It has followed me as a shadow, in my life choices and in my humour.

Ant Bush

Sefakor Aku Zikpi

Like many African women, I've had a love–hate relationship with my hair that dates back to primary school.

For most school-aged Ghanaian girls living in Australia in the 1990s, there were two choices: you either had permed hair or you did not. My sisters and I did not join the permed hair gang till relatively late, so we were for the most part of the three-plait persuasion: one plait on the left, one plait on the right and one plait in the back.

For Africans, a perm is chemical hair straightening, not chemical curling. For our mothers, in lieu of a perm, plaits or braided hair extensions were the only other way to manage our afro-textured hair. The concept of 'natural hair care' did not exist in Australia then, especially not among the relatively fledgling Ghanaian community. What the natural hair community now terms 'wash day' was a battlefield. As hard as I tried to prepare mentally for the oncoming onslaught to my scalp and entire nervous system, I could never stop myself from screaming and crying. The fear of that big black comb (every African house has a 'big black comb') raking through my afro hair sent needles of pain throughout my body. I recall my father, sitting in the corner of the room, distressed by my distress, and asking my mother to be gentler. These ordeals were the reason my mother eventually took the easy route and permed our hair some years later.

In about Grade 3 or 4, a few days before our school sports carnival, I asked my mother if I could leave my hair 'out' for the carnival. I hated my plaits. I desperately wanted two flowing, blowing-in-the-wind piggy tails, like all the other girls. I wanted to wear my hair in gold-coloured ribbons, to match the colour of my sports house, Gould.

My mother never let me wear my hair out. She always said it was 'too kenkey'. Many years later I would realise she meant 'kinky', as in tough, and not the fermented corn dough, cooked in corn husks, eaten with fish and ground pepper: a Ghanaian staple. But by some miracle, my tough-as-nails mother, who always complained about the number of combs broken in my 'kenkey' hair, agreed to let me wear my hair *out* of the plaits. Cue the Carlton dance.

The morning of the school carnival arrived. I was sitting on the floor in our lounge room, in between my mother's legs: comb on one side and green oily Dax hair pomade on the other. As she began undoing the ends of my plaits so they formed pigtails, I kept thinking, 'Melissa, Jade, Sharney, y'all better watch out cuz I'm coming through today. I'm going to have long, flowing piggy tails too.'

I didn't.

That delusion came crashing down on me at about 2.50 pm, ten minutes before the final school bell rang. We were sitting in the back field of the school.

'Her hair looks like an ant bush,' Neil Prasad, a boy in the grade above me, yelled out.

Ants don't grow on bushes, Neil, I thought. I didn't get it.

'Your hair looks like an ant bush!' he repeated, laughing.

What on God's earth was an ant bush? I knew from all the times I played in the dirt, and from all the times our kitchen was invaded by the single-file soldiers, that ants came from the ground in tiny mounds, like miniature mountains. Ants didn't come from bushes, and there were no bushes made of ants, surely. Not to my knowledge. I didn't get it.

When I did get it, I wished those dirt mounds were as big as mountains. I wished they would open up and swallow me whole. I'm not sure what stung more: Neil Prasad's comment, or the big black comb. My hair, jet black, with strands so tightly coiled they looked like the scribbles of a random doodle drawing, was no match for the humidity of a summer's day in western Sydney. My hair did not flow like Melissa's, Jade's or Sharney's. It shrivelled up, and coiled around itself, and puffed up – resembling a bush made of millions of tiny black ants.

Melissa turned to Jade and said: 'You have such pretty curls.'

Jade's response was, 'Eat the crusts on your sandwiches. My mum said it gives you curls.'

I knew I wasn't even going to try that.

The twelve-minute bus ride home was an eternity that afternoon. When I walked in the door my mother was armed with the big black comb and the tub of green Dax. She had permitted a day's grace, and not a second more. A tenth comb broke in my hair that afternoon, and as my mother lamented that this was the reason I had to keep my hair the way it always was, I realised there was something worse than having my hair in plaits: leaving it out.

Benched

Santilla Chingaipe

As far back as I can remember, I've always disliked team sports. Aside from the fact that I performed poorly in them – and spent most of the time bored, hungry and sitting on a bench – I thought I did better when my physical attributes were put to good use. And that only happened in track and field. I was very proud that I could run short distances at what I believed was a speed that rivalled Cathy Freeman's, and if I'm completely honest, it was the only thing I felt I was naturally good at. I was also obsessed with Marion Jones, of whom I'd see pictures in my mum's *Ebony* magazines. Marion Jones braided her hair just like I did, and I imagined I'd look like her when I was older and became a famous runner.

But my confidence from being good at running would take a hit every time I had to take part in cricket, softball, swimming or whatever other activity our young bodies were forced to endure in groups and under the torturous Western Australian heat. I'd protest to my parents that it was all a waste of my time, only to be met with a speech about 'the importance of learning to get along with other people'. Looking back, I think part of the reason my parents were eager for my brother and me to be involved in team sports was to fit in. We stood out, as one of the few black African working-class families in the suburb where we lived.

I decided to try my luck with my teachers.

'I don't think I should play sports, Mrs Treasurer,' I said, standing in front of her desk one day while she looked down at papers she needed to mark. She peered up at me, and then went on with her marking.

'I'm good at running, and I think that's all I should do,' I continued.

Mrs Treasurer had little patience for my rambling about how I didn't think my abilities were being adequately capitalised on. She got up and gently shooed me outside. 'Go and play with your friends. Don't forget your hat and to put on sunscreen.'

Since the adults weren't prepared to take me seriously, I decided to take matters into my eleven-year-old hands and figure out a way of absconding from sports classes. I'd been observing the Year 7s during their classes on a few occasions, and I noticed that the prefects and captains were tasked with responsibilities that forced them to 'sit out' physical activities. These included making sure there was sunscreen available, ensuring all the smaller kids behaved, chaperoning kids to the toilets, checking all the kids had hats on ... the list went on.

I devised a plan to become a prefect, and while I have no recollection of how I got elected and what my platform was, I do recall I was able to avoid most sports activities as a result, aside from the obligatory athletics carnivals.

Being a prefect was great. I had a few different sets of badges, and looked forward to assembly on Friday, when I would read out the announcements to the whole school. I felt like one of the 'big kids', and I would walk around the grounds, reprimanding kids my own age for any small thing, just so I could exercise my powers. When it was my turn to ring the recess bell, I made sure I rang it right on time.

When I was chosen as head girl the following year, my name was engraved in gold on the old school board that hung in the library, along with all these names stretching a long way back.

Mine was the only one that was different, because most people could not pronounce my first or my last name well. I was told I would be on the board forever. My parents, who were usually busy working, came down to the school that day, and they took lots of pictures and took me out for dinner at a local restaurant. My mum was very proud, and she told me she was also head girl when she was growing up, back in Zambia.

Life was going well – until we were informed that we had to take compulsory sports classes for a term. Being head girl wasn't going to get me out of this. The small suburban primary school I went to in Perth didn't have options beyond netball or AFL for winter, and I had to choose one of these to commit to for a whole term. I didn't like netball: it seemed like a 'girls' sport. I would not be caught dead playing it. Although I had friends who were girls, they didn't like the things I liked. I wanted to prove I could do what the boys did. I spent most of my childhood playing with boys; I hung around my brother and his friends, and often got into fights with boys. So I settled on AFL.

I soon discovered that I was the only girl to sign up to the team. Many of the boys took AFL very seriously and thought they'd one day play in the big leagues in Melbourne. I knew that they would assume I couldn't play because I was a girl, and would make fun of me, so I convinced two of my friends to join the team.

Although this was primary school, I was very focused. My parents helped me pick out the right kind of boots to kick a Sherrin around. Dad even watched AFL matches on television with me to help me prepare. My dad preferred soccer – or football, as he called it – and he and my brother would wake up early to catch matches on SBS. He only watched AFL if he had work on Monday, so he could have something to talk about with his colleagues.

Prior to joining the footy team, my only interactions with AFL had been the once-a-term clinics we'd have at school when a small cohort of players from the Fremantle Dockers would pay us a visit and hand out inflatable footballs and t-shirts. I knew girls didn't play the sport, because there were none on TV.

I still recall the rush of adrenaline when I was taught, in my first training session, how to kick a football properly. Most of the boys already played footy during lunch and recess, but it was all new to me. My coach pulled me aside and walked me to the front of the goal posts. I remember him instructing me to hold the ball with my arms stretched out and my eye on the goal, running and then letting go of the ball midair so that my foot could pick it up and kick it. My kicks barely went further than 20 metres, but I was still proud of myself. I could play this boys' sport.

From then on, I'd look forward to AFL practice every week. My friends soon gave up, and it was just me and the boys. My kicks and handballs never improved, and I'd run away anytime I'd see someone attempt a mark near me. I vividly recall one of the boys losing his two front teeth after taking a knock, and I was not interested in experiencing that.

After what seemed like a lifetime of practice sessions, our team took part in a championship with other local schools. We played every weekend, and I was always on the bench. One day, my coach told me I would be starting in the next match. I was so excited I told my parents it could be a life-changing game. I'd watched *The Mighty Ducks* so many times I began to believe that somehow the skills that had escaped me during practice would suddenly appear, and I'd kick the match-winning goal and go on to play for the Fremantle Dockers. Although the Eagles were the Western Australian team that won premierships in the 1990s, I'd convinced myself that I would be the star the Dockers had been waiting for to lead them to glory. I could hear the commentators saying, 'It's Chingaipe with the ball. With only seconds left before the siren goes off, and the Dockers are behind by two points ... She's going for goal. Can she do it? She's going for it. She's going ... oh, it's *in*. Chingaipe scores the match-winning goal! You beaaaaauty! And there it is: Dockers win by four points.'

A few minutes after the match started, my coach yelled out to me to remember who to pass the ball to. I was not required to do any more than that. This seemed easy enough, and once I got comfortable, I thought, I would show the coach what I was truly capable of.

While I was daydreaming about what that moment would feel like, I was quickly reminded of my immediate reality when I heard a thud near me. I turned around and realised that the ball had been kicked towards me and wasn't in anyone's possession. Before I could think, I saw a pack of boys running aggressively towards me. I picked up the ball and, somewhere in the distance, I could hear my coach yelling for me to pass it. The pack of boys moved closer, looking scarier than I had imagined they would, in my dreams of this game. I panicked, dropping the ball like a hot potato. I jumped aside and watched as this pack of boys fell on top of one another, trying to grab the Sherrin.

Feeling relieved that I'd just avoided certain death, I turned to look at my coach, who pulled me aside and told me to sit out the rest of the match. A few of the kids laughed at me and, as I sat back on the bench, I realised that maybe AFL wasn't my game after all.

I spent the rest of the season on the bench, and never played a game again. But what I did learn from my short-lived football career was the importance of having a go. Playing AFL – albeit briefly – taught me that there's nothing that boys can do that I can't, and I've carried that lesson with me into adulthood. And I still *hate* taking part in team sports.

How to Be a Green Monster

Cath Moore

There I am. In that old black-and-white passport-sized photo, perched on my mother's knee, wide-eyed and waiting.

Back in 1977, babies didn't have their own passports. But I've seen my Guyanese birth certificate. All the details have been written sideways by a left-handed registrar.

Wedged between Venezuela and Suriname, Guyana is a nation in South America, but also part of the Caribbean. It's where my father was born way back in 1937. And what do I have left of it now? It's my birthplace but not my homeland.

If I played the quiz show of my life, I'd probably get half the answers wrong. Guyana is the place Demerara sugar comes from and where the Jonestown mass suicide happened. It makes me ashamed that what I know about Guyana is random and impersonal. Found facts and muted feelings. Still, I'm nostalgic about a place of which I have no memory – only other people's recollections of a time and space long since disappeared.

We move to America in 1976, a period in which racial tensions are high. Back in Guyana, my mother, with her blonde hair and blue eyes, was accused of 'stealing' my dad away from his community. As one half of a mixed-race couple down south in Georgia, she is met with similar suspicion. The seeds of otherness have been planted long before I understand what it means to be dark-skinned in Australia.

That picture with me on my mother's knee provides safe

passage to Sydney in 1978. Mum has run away from it all – Catholicism, sexism, parochialism – only to land right back where she was born and bred.

My Irish grandfather, Richard Boylan, was a publican, and moved the family up to the Blue Mountains and Cowra before coming back to Sydney's northern suburbs. Old photo albums browning round the edge keep the record of my early years there. Up at Uncle Johnnie's place on Eastwood Avenue, surrounded by a wonderfully loud and expansive brood of Mum's cousins, some still with an Irish brogue that tickles their vowels. Gone is the blackness of my father, who I will not see for another twenty years. These are my people now.

This is the time I like myself the most, before I know what colour means. When the lightbulb of consciousness switches on at around four years old, I don't see my skin. I see the family I have been raised with and I assume that I am white, just like them. Safe in my mother's land.

In 1979, Mum gets an academic job interstate and we move into university housing in Canberra. Scholars from all over the world – Papua New Guinea, Poland, Denmark, India, Kenya, Peru, Canada, Pakistan – live in Carroll Street with their families. They bring myriad colours and accents with them.

There's another photo, of my fifth birthday party. In the backyard, grown-ups in bell-bottoms drink Coolabah cask wine, and a rainbow of kids in terry-towelling jumpsuits dip their plastic spoons into packets of Wizz Fizz. In Carroll Street, ethnic diversity is normalised. We run through one another's back doors and take whatever food is on offer: injera one day, Vegemite 'worms' in Vita-Weats the next. We celebrate Guy Fawkes Day, Diwali and Halloween, and you are the odd one out if you 'come' from Australia. We live in our own little United

Nations bubble, separate from the white middle-classness of 1980s Canberra.

Australia's 'multicultural melting pot' is a civilising notion constructed by idealists, watching the experiment unfold from a safe distance. How does it feel to be lumped into this category, under this term, thrown around by policymakers protected by the privilege of colonial whiteness? It is okay if your family are all the same colour. But a single white woman with a brown kid? Outside of Carroll Street I often catch a stranger's furtive, accusatory glance. *Not Aboriginal. Then what – adopted?* It feels like we have been charged with conspiracy to commit fraud and are perpetually awaiting trial. Whenever I pass an Aboriginal face in the street, as uncommon as that is, I hope for some kind of reassuring transaction: 'You're okay. I see your shame. I feel it too.' Do they hear my silent offering? Can I seek kinship here? I often think so, whether this is real or imagined.

....

It is certainly rare to see African faces in Canberra as I grow up. With no reference points for my dad's existence, he becomes even more of an alien concept. I love going to my schoolfriend KB's house because she has a proper family: mother, father and siblings. All the same colour. I take it all in; the smell, sight, taste, touch and sound of a real family are intoxicating. Will it rub off on me if I stay a little longer?

My mum befriended a family from Guyana once. The girl, Nadia, was my age, and we were so proud we'd found each other. We sat in her room one day with a cassette deck recording our simplistic anthem of solidarity: 'We've got brown eyes, brown eyes. And we've got brown skin, brown skin. And we both come from … the Caribbean.' Then we ran down to the playground near her house. A group of boys called us 'niggers'. Our simple joy and sense of belonging in the world was gone. Shame sat heavy in our stomachs as we walked home. Not a word spoken between us.

When I am about ten, Mum comes to school one day. She calls out my name, but I pretend not to hear. Her presence embarrasses me; kids ask how I can be brown if she isn't. It's then that I really see my skin. My father has made me visible in the worst possible way. I hate him and I hate myself.

I especially hate my dark lip hair. 'You've got a moustache!' others say. I am miserable, and in class my hand hovers around the offending area. Mum gets hair removal cream; it's stinky and messy, but I do not want the legacy my father has given me.

And the craving for whiteness begins.

The first and most desirable form I crave is mother white-ness. I covet my mum's long blonde hair. I resist my own tangle of fuzzy curls, tie it up into a bun, away and out of sight. Mum wants to see it, tells me that it's beautiful. It's okay for her – the brush goes straight through her shiny golden mane.

The second form is waiting-room whiteness. This is a cloak of invisibility that shields you from penetration when you walk into a specialist's office. When I enter without the cloak, every-one looks up from their trashy mag and stares.

Third is the pretty whiteness that permeates every single television show and cover of *Woman's Day*: 'our' Nicole, Cate, Rebecca, Tracey. How brave, talented and beautiful they are. The screen and page reiterate who's really important. I want to turn inside out, show everyone that whiteness lives inside me, too.

It's at school where the fear and ignorance of adulthood reso-nate the loudest. A boy rides past and calls me a sambo. Mum, my fierce protector, chases him down, gives him a talking-to. I can't hear what Mum says, but the boy looks over and stares straight through me. I am nothing to him, but have caused trouble all the same.

At a music camp, someone makes a joke about my hair and Velcro. Kids look at me as the punchline hits. They want me to smile, to be strangely complicit in the humiliation.

On a trip to Katoomba, two teenage boys make monkey sounds at me. I try to focus on the Three Sisters behind them. We've come here to look at the wondrous rock formations.

The boys tell me to go back to Africa. I do not have the words and the confidence to explain: 'I'm not from Africa. And Guyana is not the same country as Ghana. Although my father did work there, as a physics teacher. This is where my middle name, Akosua, comes from. It means "Sunday's child". I was actually born on a Thursday, but Mum did not like the name Yaa. Being African means lots of things and speaks to many places and people outside the continent. So go fuck yourselves.'

I have both the words and the confidence now. But I cannot go back and help that little brown girl.

....

I grow into a teenager. Both self-conscious and self-assured in my hormone-fuelled becoming. On the way to what, I am not yet sure.

Alfred Deakin High School in the late 1980s – what a mess of heavy metal t-shirts, permed or peroxided hair, and stone-washed jeans. My motley crew of friends wear trench coats and Doc Martens. We listen to the Violent Femmes as we wallow in teenage angst. Everyone is busy trying to keep their heads above water, and I stay under the radar.

In Year 7, I tamed my curls with a handful of gel and, just to make sure the fuzz fully complied, stuck a handful of coloured hairclips on top. Candy head. But in Year 10 the hair comes out.

My hair has always been a conspicuous marker of difference. Untamed, unruly, unrepentant. Can I feel differently about it? Can I really embrace what my father has given me? Letting my hair out is a quiet rebellion. I am testing myself, as well as the world at large. *Go on, what about it?*

There I am in my high-school photo, a mane of thick curls loose and on display for the first time. 'Cool hair' is the caption by my name in the yearbook.

I am compared to Yannick Noah, the French tennis player, and more often to Lucy, a character from the television show *Degrassi Junior High*. I don't mind. Being compared to a figure on television is validating.

I catch the bus after school to tennis lessons with my friend Michelle and her brother Rickard. He is colourblind, and we often joke that through his eyes, I might appear green. A green monster. It never seems like a racist taunt. Given his bright red hair and a pronounced underbite that will eventually have to be reconstructed, I'm sure Rickard has been the butt of many jokes too.

When I turn eighteen, there's sex, drugs and rock'n'roll aplenty at the Australian National University. Now my Afro-Caribbean heritage and womanly curves make me desirable. 'Don't you see it though? I'm whiter than sliced bread underneath!' I want to tell people. It leaves me feeling empowered to provide some kind of rite of passage for those middle-class white boys who have never left the nest of old money, security and tradition. Exoticism affords me an authority I've never had before. I don't deny it, nor am I ashamed. I am not a victim. We are all playing games as we move from becoming to finally and undoubtedly being.

That provocateur is twenty years older now.

Somewhere along the way I find my father. Too late for the little brown girl who feared him but missed him all the same.

After decades apart, I remember 'meeting' him for the first time. 'Hi, Dad. There you are,' I said. Like it had always been. Many fractured lives blend approximate truths and wishful thinking into something resembling 'the past'. Now I have a witness who can lead me back to that first breath, skyward gaze, footfall on Guyanese soil.

I've only just looked at that part of myself in the mirror. Let the woman who stares back reconcile what her skin really means. Australia is a land of (im)migrants lost and found en route to a patchwork population of comers and goers. A place where layers of the past can either be stripped away completely or end up sinking deeper into the fabric of life. The markers of heritage can change radically. What is shameful in childhood is, for an adult, liberating. Or vice versa, depending on which path fate guides you down.

I don't know if Australia is any less racist than it was when I was growing up. I did, however, feel certain that when I had a child they would share my colouring, and would never have to explain themselves as I had often done. As it turns out, my boy has straight blond hair and pale skin. In the playground at his school I'm asked the same question again: 'Why are you two different colours?' But this time, I crouch down and explain that my boy's skin comes from Germany, Ireland and Guyana. I wax lyrical about the wonders of genetics until the curious kid just wants to go play again.

The question 'where do you come from?' is for many people inherently divisive because the subtext speaks so loudly – you cannot be from here, and are therefore Other. But the opposite of otherness is to be known. I went looking for Australian women connected to the African diaspora. I wanted to see them, to be known by them and for them to know me. We talk; we create new conversations. I testify on a regular basis to my former selves that were denied, ridiculed and rejected.

Some people think that, by embracing my Afro-Caribbean heritage in middle age, I'm trying to jump on board a train that is not mine to ride. Does denial, or acceptance, make me a fraud? I don't identify as 'Australian' because I still don't know what lies beneath the myths to which we cling. Unreconciled with the past, our nation's collective psyche is damaged.

Growing up, I found it near impossible to engage with any culture apart from my Anglo-Irish heritage, which was accepted as part of a wider Australian identity. But if you're persistent and deep dig enough, the roots can be uncovered. Now I'm finding mythical creatures within Afro-Guyanese folklore, like Mr Nancy the spider man, considered to be the spirit of knowledge in African stories. This feels real to me, a cultural legacy I can pass on.

I can still hear 'The Brown-eyed Girls' in my head. That tediously repetitive song I wrote with Nadia, the only other Guyanese kid I ever met, who understood how you could be proud and lost in equal measure. I sometimes wonder if she remembers walking home from the playground that day, or if it's all part of a past she'd rather forget.

But there are other songs now, too. My son's school always plays music through the loudspeakers just before the morning bell. One day, I hear a tinny steel drum, dancing on the back of the wind, calling us forward towards the school gates. 'Listen,' I say to my boy. 'This is Grandpa's music from the Caribbean. It's called calypso.' I want a loudspeaker myself. 'Stop, everyone! Stop and listen to the joy it brings,' I'd say.

WELCOME TO
AUSTRALIA

New Life

Iman Sissay

EL-GADARIF, SUDAN

I think my mother is going to die tonight.

It begins with no light. My siblings and I hear people yelling and running, as if there is some kind of disaster – an apocalypse, maybe. There is an odd wailing, almost like a howl, that comes intermittently. My siblings and I start to panic. We run up and down stairs in the brownstone building, trying to find our parents. We don't know where we're going, but we want to escape the unilluminated premises and the horrible sound.

I have always found our house strange: the doors don't close, and the windows are almost the same length and height as the doors. Not that it matters – my family sleep outside more than inside. I don't understand why we do this when we have a perfectly adequate house, but possibly it's due to how cavernous the building feels without lights and furniture. My siblings and I never complain, though; we love every moment of it. I fall asleep counting stars, and watching planes pass through the clouds, and I set my mind to where they might be travelling. I think my siblings do the same.

My sister and I lose our brothers while pounding up and down stairs in our desire to find the front door and escape the house. We stumble upon our mother in a room surrounded by people, our neighbours. She has tears running down her face. She looks to be in agony. We are confused. My sister's face becomes doleful, but we maintain our childish stances, unsure what to do, how to react.

My dad becomes aware of our presence. He guides us outside without explanation. We sit there with the distant screams and the howls of pain in our ears. I am grateful for the wintry wind gusting over me bitterly, stopping my brain from functioning.

Soon it is quiet, the night sleepy and silent again.

We don't understand how the whole birth process works, as we've never witnessed it firsthand before. My mother was never dangerously ill. She was just in extreme pain.

Hours later, the frightening night becomes beautiful, because a new life is born.

KHARTOUM, SUDAN

I'm curling my toes in frustration at the wave of heat that envelops the bus. It is scorching: no air conditioning at all. Snatches of the vibrant, mismatched rags most of the passengers wear shine in the window's glare. The chattering between strangers is constant; the people pull exaggerated faces and roll eyes at one another. I feel as though we have been relocated to a new planet. Outside, the ground is flaky, covered with a weak, dirty, reddish sand. There's a complete lack of vegetation, and were it not for the buckets of water hanging on the bus's chassis, I would wonder how we could possibly survive this long road trip.

I sleep fitfully, and I'm glad I do, because when I awaken with a breeze I am in a less daunting environment.

We're now in a city. We arrive at a building, where we enter a large room. I gradually realise that there are about fifty bunkbeds in it. It soon becomes clear that everyone is distressed by our accommodation, largely because of its complete lack of privacy.

Beside me, a mother and her daughter are arguing about something that's probably very minor and has been exaggerated by the tension of the situation. Outside are hundreds more people who have packed up their lives and reduced their houses to baggage to escape Sudan.

My mum, my two sisters and I gather together with our bags and belongings. My dad and brothers are in the men's camp. My younger sister and I sneak over there to see them. We find our way there, following the palm trees, and are annoyed to discover that for some reason their camp seems to be more luxurious than the women's.

It seems the only time the whole family gets together is for meals. We always eat the same traditional lunch: cooked beans with salad and bread. The beans are seasoned by a combination of boiled egg and oil. Then, every day after lunch, we explore Khartoum, the city we're in.

Sometimes a lady shows up at unpredictable times to teach us a new language, which we all find exciting. She teaches us the alphabet, and how to count from one to fifty, in English, but by the next day we always forget what she has taught us.

I can't comprehend how the whole process works, but I know we are here in this city because we are going to move to Australia.

When it is time to leave the ridiculous heat of Khartoum, there are goodbyes. Families hug and cry their farewells, as buses take one group after another. My parents are emotional, especially my mum.

I wonder now how my goodbyes might have been different if I had known I was never going to see these people again.

We get on the bus appointed for us, and wave through the smudged window at those left behind.

An Ethiopian couple approach us with a middle-aged Australian woman. They are a part of Central Care, a volunteer-run organisation, and are helping us meet our new situation. When they drive us to our new address, I never let my eyes fall – not even though my brain is terribly jetlagged. I don't want to miss anything, because already I have a strange fear of forgetting these defining moments.

Soon I find myself in a room, indescribably rich to my eyes, and I am surrounded by toys. I even notice a pair of fairy wings hanging from a bronze mantle. I hear my siblings running blithely. I can't understand how they have so much energy.

I give in to temptation and drag myself to a curiously shaped plaything smothered in acres of buttons. I start pressing at them all, and they begin to make melodies and sounds.

My sister must hear the noise because she bursts in and snatches it from me. I don't get mad; instead I find myself another musical toy, even more kooky than the other.

We spend the next couple of days endeavouring to get comfortable in our new home, amid all this unimaginable property.

....

The following Monday, my family and I stand together in green and yellow and smile as Gina, one of Central Care's volunteers, takes a picture of us in these lively colours. Two of my siblings and I wave goodbye to our parents and baby sister, then get in a car that's vibrantly red, travelling to another new beginning.

We arrive at a vast school, where we are separated and put in different buildings: my sister in kindergarten, me in lower primary school, my brother in a higher grade. A teacher asks me questions: 'How are you? What's your name? How old are you?' I have this feeling she's testing my English. In truth, I only understand a few words, so I stay quiet as Gina gives my name and age, then leaves to settle my sister and brother.

My eyes drift to the walls, which are covered with drawings, numbers and letters. In a corner, not far from me, there is a small kitchen with plastic items – even plastic food. The ceiling has threads of string running from one end to the other. Along those threads run pictures and shapes.

My teacher introduces to me to two girls: Katie, with blonde hair, and Nikita, with red. I can't stop staring at Nikita. Back in Sudan, no one would know a person with red hair could exist. I think she might have powers. My teacher grabs a bell from the desk beside her, and I watch her ring it at least three times. Everyone begins to lower their voices, and in seconds the classroom is quiet.

I don't understand what the teacher is saying, but I have a feeling it is about me – the other kids are staring at me with a variety of expressions. Some seem excited, some curious. Others just sit there unbothered.

I don't like the attention. I want to cry; I want to go home.

Finally, a loud sound pierces my ears. I have no idea where it comes from. I see all the other kids running to the adjoining room, to their bags, and seizing their food.

I am shown to my bag by two teachers and pull an apple and a chocolate bar out of my lunch box. What a strange combination for someone used to eating a savoury meal.

But Katie and Nikita sit with me outside while we all eat our food. After that they show me to the playground, which is exciting because of how colourful and fun it looks. We spend recess hanging out in the playground, and I want to stay there forever.

I sit only a few centimetres away from the television, and watch, enthralled, as the human fish swim away from the octopus. I find it so exciting and bizarre; I can't help but wonder if such creatures really exist in the ocean. I ask my father, expecting him to laugh and enquire why I think something so peculiar exists. But instead he tells me that they are scarier in real life, that they take little kids and lock them up under the sea, then turn them into fish. I wait for him to break the lie with a smile but he doesn't, and all week I have nightmares about evil sea creatures.

When the weekend comes, Jane, another Central Care volunteer, takes us to the beach. We are all very excited about this excursion to Bellerive – my first time at an Australian beach – but I can't help but think about what my dad has told me.

When we arrive at the wide sandy crescent, I admire the combination of the sand, ocean and sun; they complement one another so well, just like colours in a painting. The ocean is sparkling, and from a distance it looks as though it is filled with diamonds. As we walk towards the water, the percussion of the waves sounds, our kid footsteps along with it. I rumple my toes, feeling the soft and balmy shore. I start to dig a hole with my toes because of how comforting the sand is. I watch kids and adults swim and run around. I can't wait to encounter the same feeling of freedom.

Jane starts to walk me and my siblings towards the marina, but as we get closer my fear grows. My brothers start racing towards the water. I watch them freak out at its touch and then sprint back in again. When my sister and I finally reach the water, it is gentle, not like what I expected, and we wade in. I glance around to see that no one is getting attacked or dragged under by any type of sea creature. I realise that my dad was lying with that terrifying tale.

Every year at this time, I wake up with nothing but the feeling of glorious contentment. My dad always starts the day by greeting us with the same words: 'Eid Mubarak.' This announces the end of the fast. It's the only time my body wants to get up – usually during Ramadan I feel weighed down, as though I am wearing a thick coat five times my size, exhausted by fasting and by the prospect of more days without food. But this day is meant to be celebrated with enthusiasm and passion by all Muslims, and so it will be.

When I leave my room, I smell all variety of spices and ingredients, and my body sings, though I know the food will have to wait. We have our baths and dress in our Eid clothes, bright and gaudy, with accessories, to show our fervour warmly and with pride.

Our breakfast is dates, and all sorts of sweets and chocolate. I don't care if it's the unhealthiest thing for breakfast: it's Eid. My siblings and I stuff it all down, until my mum takes the chocolates and hides them, to save some for the guests – though we know where she stashes them. Then the sounds of drums, chants and shouts greet our ears as my mum puts on some Sudanese music. The journey – the heat of Khartoum, the staring faces in the classroom, the Bellerive monsters – has been worth it. The pain has brought new life.

Idle Thoughts

Khalid Warsame

So, the other day I was telling a white friend of mine an anecdote about this funny thing that happened when I used to work at Big W as a teenager and in the telling of this story I made passing mention of this other time that I got jumped on my way home from work, which was, to me, slightly incidental to the main story, but it shocked her – like, actually shocked her – and she's like, 'I can't believe that happened! Were you okay?' and I replied that, yeah, I was winded a bit and I got a split lip and a couple of bruises and I vomited on my way home but other than that I was fine, and then she's like, 'Did you at least go to the police?' and I was momentarily thrown by this question, to be honest, because I didn't think going to the police was ever an option, back then or now – I mean: yeah, I guess I could have gone to the cops, and yeah, I knew who those guys were, but I've only ever had three interactions with police all my life and the first was when I was just a kid and in my uncle's car in Flemington and police pulled us over and my uncle got into an argument with this big red-faced guy whose name was probably something real broad like Constable Steve or something, and the second was with this old guy they had at my primary school who taught us African kids life skills that never really stuck – stuff like obeying traffic signals and riding a bicycle and respecting authority – but who also pronounced Hyundai wrong (like '*high*-yun-dai' instead of 'hee-*yun*-day') and I guess I never really got over that, which

I suspect is what set me up for a lifetime of minor traffic violations, and the *third* time was when I was fourteen and these two cops wordlessly chucked me into the back of a divvy van because some security guard at Werribee Plaza suspected us of, you know, whatever, and me and my mates got hauled in and, yeah, I kind of mouthed off to them because they wanted me to empty my pockets and I had fifty bucks in there that I was really fond of and, yeah, we *were* kind of skipping school.

So I spent the entire day in an interview room while this guy, who I hated then and still hate now, mouthed off to me about how I was worthless and a shit-bag, which was way out of line because, *damn*, I was fourteen – and I'm just sitting there taking it because he wanted me to call my parents and there's no way in hell I'm exposing myself to enfilade fire from both ends of this trench I've found myself in, so my plan was to just sit around until it got reasonably late and I could be reasonably certain that my old man was at the social club on Boundary Road chatting with his mates about politics and good-old-days type stuff and then call my mum – my mum, by the way, dispenses with forgiveness like an eleventh-century Catholic bishop in a buyer's market, so she's definitely the one I want to break me out of this joint.

By the time I get let out it's nine and my mum is in tears because, shit, now she's got *two* boys who are veering off the path and I was supposed to be the good one and now I'm just wallowing there doing what I can to seem small and insignificant and no boy on this hot earth wants to make his mother cry, and here's the thing: I guess I just avoided cops from then on because I heard the stories (Ahmed from back in North Melbourne got all his front teeth knocked out for no reason, and the shaykh's son got called a 'bloody Osama' for wearing his Friday best,

79

and everyone gets followed by an unmarked Holden with thick antennas driven by square-faced men), and now that I had the firsthand experience, cops were the last thing on my mind – and there it is: I guess I didn't realise how completely my experiences differ from those of my friend from the beginning of this story, because what we're talking about here are two fundamentally different worldviews, and as I get older I'm noticing that a much higher percentage of white kids grow up and basically do okay compared to the too many Somali boys who I grew up with who just kind of fell off the 'Do Well' truck – some are in jail, others are caught in black holes of troubles, but most are just lost: no job, no prospects, and no real idea. And whose fault is it? A lot of folk buy into this sense of self-determination – that they're actually responsible for their own successes in life. It's a complete load of shit, you know? Ask any coloured kid in any city, ask any Indigenous person, any woman in academia, ask anyone who isn't straight and white and middle class – there's a system. A system that is invested in the success,of some and not of others; and you've got to be blind not to notice it.

There was this kid we called Qantas who lived over in the Sutton Street flats with his aunt (North Melbourne, late nineties, you get the idea) who showed up at *dugsi* (Sunday school) one day, where we were learning to memorise the Qur'an not because we wanted to but because our mothers would slap us across our butts and our *macalins* would sting us across the palm with a switch if we didn't, which was a really inefficient method of instruction, by the way, because I barely remember any surahs but I still find myself evaluating the odd branch for its potential as an implement of pedagogy – so Qantas was this new kid, right, who was fresh as the morning sun when he showed up at *dugsi* for the first time and he had that wild uncombed look about him that we settled school-going kids really envied at the time but I now know to be related to the fact that about a third of Somali kids I grew up with lost their fathers to the war, meaning Qantas probably didn't have a real flash childhood as a result – but kids don't notice that sort of thing at all, and we were just really impressed with his all-hours roaming attitude and the fact that he spoke Somali with an untouchable fluency that sprang from his tongue fully formed and that he had this grave old voice that made him seem older than his visa age, which probably wasn't his real age anyway, so Skinny gave him the name Qantas because that was one of the few English words he knew when we interrogated him about his origins, and he waxed a little too lyrically about his plane journey for us not to wield it against him and, besides, the way he was dressed made it really easy to poke fun at his FOB-ness: polyester shirt and sarong (called a *macawis*) and leather sandals and, yeah, a fan of thickly curled hair that sprang out of his head like a crown – he had talents, though: talking to him even for a moment, you could tell this guy was whip-smart, you could tell that something up there was switched on – and he was driven too: damn near raised himself and had no family to look out for him.

Qantas must be in his late twenties now, and last I heard of the dude, he wasn't doing too well for those symptomatic reasons: he could never really get the hang of school, he could never really get the hang of Australia, and he could never really summit the important peaks of adjustment. If he had the right environment, if he had a little help getting up on, well, idle thoughts, aren't they.

The Long Way Home

Guido Melo

Rio

Salvador is the blackest city in Brazil. It's where I was born, in 1976. Salvador is about seventy per cent black and thirty per cent white. I would compare it to a southern state in the United States – Mississippi, perhaps – because the thirty per cent run everything. They own all the businesses and have all the power.

My father was in the air force. His position shielded me from a lot of racism, but 'shielded from' doesn't mean eliminated: I suffered from it throughout my childhood.

I don't remember having any conversations about racism with my parents when I was growing up, but I remember listening to a lot of protest music. My memories of my father from that time are of him reading a lot of newspapers and listening to a lot of vinyl. I remember my parents always telling me: 'We are black; black people have to be careful, have to be aware.' It was like a mantra for them.

I only had one year at school in Salvador, because in 1984, we moved to Rio de Janeiro, where my father had been transferred. He was a meteorologist: he worked in the airport towers and would give the weather report to those operating and directing the planes. His job was very important: any aeroplane flying in or out of Rio would go through him.

We flew into Rio in an Avro, an old English aeroplane.

We arrived at night, around 9.00 pm, and I still remember looking out the window at the lights below, the sheer size of the city spread out below me. It was the first time I'd flown. Flying was expensive back in the 1980s. We were probably lower middle class and, in fact, even for middle-class Brazilians, flying was a big deal. None of my friends had flown; no one I knew had flown.

The smell once we landed into Rio was foul. I'd lived near the beach in Salvador, but this was different – I could smell Guanabara Bay. The bay is kind of like Sydney Harbour, but back then it was very dirty. It had this odour of sewage mixed with algae.

We arrived in August or July, and we had nowhere to go, so we lived in this hotel for six months, in one room. I think there were six of us at that time, including my mum and dad. Having hotel food every day was fantastic.

The mornings would start with Mum washing the family's clothes, and we would go to the rooftop to hang them out. I would be playing with my plastic aeroplane full of shells – the shells were the passengers. I liked to do air crashes. The shells that stayed in the plane were the passengers who survived, and the shells that fell out were dead people.

Then we would go downstairs to a park, which was full of agoutis – they're like giant guinea pigs. It was in the centre of Rio, so it was busy. We would play with the agoutis and listen to music.

We moved to Rio halfway through the school year, so I had to repeat Grade 1. That shaped my entire life. I've always been older than my friends because of this. Maybe I'd even say I matured later.

Children in Rio were crueller than in Salvador – or perhaps I was just more aware of racism by then. My first memory of racism involved a classmate who wouldn't lend me her eraser. She said it was 'because you're black'.

At first I was very naive, very nice, very honest. I got corrupted by the other kids. The local kids would steal my toys. They would beat me up for no reason. There was probably an element of racism to this: they were all white kids.

My mum got angry. She used to tell me, 'If someone punches you, or does anything to you, throw rocks at them.' This was Brazil; it was much rougher than Australia. I think it is fair to point out that my mother had a rough upbringing of her own. Fighting was one of the only things she knew. In Stan Grant's *Talking to My Country*, he mentions that one of the main lessons he learnt from his father was 'whenever outnumbered in a fight ... get in front of a wall so [as not to be] surrounded'. When I read this, it resonated with me. It made sense. You were taught to be violent, and violence was all around you.

I remember this kid beat me up when I was about nine. I said, 'If you beat me again, I will break your window.'

He said, 'You're not going to break my window. You wouldn't dare.'

When he beat me again, I got some rocks, went to his house and broke his window. His parents were mad. There was an argument between his parents and mine – lots of yelling, probably some shoving. They were a white family, of course.

Over time I grew up. I was smart. I learnt more about racism, and I learnt to fight against it. But it takes a long time. It takes a *lifetime*. I'm still learning today.

I picked up English through songs. My father used to sing English songs. He was never a Rolling Stones guy; he preferred the Beatles. At thirteen, I realised I could learn English very easily. There were these music magazines with the song lyrics, and I memorised them all. By fourteen, I could hold short conversations. Later on, I learnt English at school, but only for a couple of hours a week. Most of what I learnt, I picked up myself using this method.

I think you dream just for something bigger than what you have. If you live in a cave, your dream is to get out of the cave. If you live on an island, your dream is to get off the island. I just wanted to be wealthier. Capitalism and structural racism sells it to you that all you need to do is work hard; that if you're wealthier, racism will be erased. I lived on a beautiful island in Rio. There were bananas and guavas hanging from the trees, but I wanted to live in Ipanema or Copacabana. That's a dream I've achieved now – when I go back to Brazil, I stay in Ipanema. I'm a bit of a local there now. But you know, sometimes when your dreams come true you realise that's not what you really wanted.

Rio's a hub. To practise my English, I started talking to foreigners. There was this place called Lapa where all the bohemians would go – you know, people who lived alternative lifestyles. I'd realised by then that I didn't fit in with mainstream society. I'd go there, and listen to their ideas and talk to them about life.

In 1990s Rio, if you were middle class you had to hang around white people, so even if you knew black people, eventually all those you hung out with – even dated – would be white. It sounds so surreal now. My school had 5000 students, and 4900 of them were white. I just tried to survive. Some people accuse Sammy Davis Jnr being a sell-out, but when you think about it, he started work when he was around three, and all the people he worked for were white, the people he entertained were white. You learn one thing: if I hang with them, I will survive.

Of course, I'm far from being Sammy Davis Jnr, but I think, with hindsight, all 100 of us at that school thought we should be as far from each other as possible, because with two of us people would feel intimidated. I remember watching one of those spoof movies that makes fun of cinema tropes. A black guy turns up at a party, and there is already a black guy there, and he says to him, 'Oh, it was you who was supposed to come today. I thought it was me! My bad. I'm leaving now. You can stay.' During the 1980s and 1990s, there was one black person at any social gathering, so people could say 'we're not racist'. That's how it felt for me. If I saw a black guy at a party, I would walk the other way. It's awful. It's painful to admit that. In fact, this is the first time I ever have.

I started to hang around with a lot of artists. They were very left-leaning. In 1997, I realised the university near me had the best computers in Rio. I saw a few black students on campus. So I would dress up as nice as I could – given my financial limitations – and walk right up to the door of the computer lab. The security guards would look at me and think I was a student. I would spend the whole day on the internet learning things, and I soon would sneak into whatever classes I could. I took philosophy, politics … heaps of different classes; there was nothing to lose. Some of the teachers even liked me, because I showed up and wanted to learn.

All I knew was white people. I wanted to hang out with them and be accepted.

PARIS

I was working as a computer and printer repairer, and a Parisian friend I'd met in Rio invited me to go to France. I had enough money to either buy a second-hand car or get a plane ticket to Paris. The car would have helped me. If I had a car, I could have travelled for work and earnt more money, to set up my life in Brazil. But instead I chose yolo (you only live once). I went yolo before yolo existed. I went to Paris!

I arrived at Charles de Gaulle on 14 September 2001, four days after my twenty-fifth birthday. My original flight was booked for 12 September, but it was cancelled, because the world landscape had dramatically changed the day before. I knew a tiny bit of French, because I'd done a course in Brazil, but languages come very easily to me: I spent a week in Paris, and by the Friday, I was fluent.

In Paris, for the first time in my life, I was treated as a man. '*Bonjour, monsieur*,' people would address me. That was impressive. It was so nice. '*Bonjour, monsieur*,' I would reply. I don't know if that Paris exists anymore, but in 2001, in my Paris, everyone said hello to me on the streets.

I stayed for about four months. When I came back, the first thing I said to my dad, when I saw him at the airport, was 'I will never live in Brazil again.'

I didn't embark on a mission to get out of Brazil. It wasn't a masterplan, but I was very open about my desire to leave, and actively sought opportunities to do so. I tried to get a job on a cruise ship. I was rejected continually, and I can only think it was because I was a black man, because by that time I spoke three languages. I was an eager 25-year-old black man who spoke French, Portuguese and English, and I could not get the gig, no matter how hard I tried.

Then I met my partner. She was Australian. We worked together for eight months in Rio. She needed to go back to Melbourne to finish her degree, and she said, 'Do you want to come with me, and see how it goes?' I said yes, but before I moved to Australia, I needed to see Paris one more time.

At the airport in Lisbon, when I had left Brazil behind, I started speaking English for some reason. I thought, *He's just going to be racist to me anyway, so I may as well speak English*. I was already on the defensive. These are the things that form you in Brazil: you don't know who is going to attack you, so you're always on edge. I had to explain why I was going to Australia, why I was travelling alone on a one-way ticket. The immigration official said to me, 'I know your kind. I know what you're up to. But you're going to Paris. I'm going to let you pass. You're going to be their problem now.' I don't think he ever believed that I was going to Australia.

When I got to Paris, Bush had just declared war on Iraq. There was a huge protest in the centre of the city, and I went along. I met up with friends. It was snowing. It was beautiful.

PERTH

After about eighty hours in Paris, I boarded a plane to Australia. The flight path took me to Perth. My partner wasn't arriving in Melbourne for another four days. I didn't want to get there before her, so I had planned a four-day stopover in Perth.

When I landed, I was expecting anything but help, given my experience at the Lisbon airport. The immigration officer asked me why I was coming to Australia. I said because of my partner.

She asked, 'Where are you going to?'

'Melbourne.'

'How long will you be staying?'

'Probably indefinitely. Hopefully.'

Then she looked at me and smiled, this white lady, and said, 'Welcome to Australia.'

It's the simple things, you know. I thought, *I have arrived in a good place.*

Perth was very undeveloped at the time, at least in my mind. I think I remember red dirt, this red dirt everywhere, but then memory is so strange and unreliable.

I was going to stay in a backpacker hostel. I overheard these two English guys talking: they were going to the same place. I pushed my way into the conversation and said, 'Let's go together.' They didn't want to. They told me that my bags wouldn't fit in the car, but I was insistent: I said that I could hold them in my lap. That was very Brazilian of me. I don't think I would do that today. I was interested in being their friend, but they weren't interested in me. We shared the ride, we shook hands and we went our separate ways.

I put my bag in the room and changed into shorts. It was February, summer in Perth – incredibly blue skies, this dry heat I had never felt before. There were flies. It was all very new to me. There were no smartphones then, so there was nothing to do but explore on foot. I walked around for a few hours. I was scanning, literally scanning, the streets for black people. I'd never felt like such a minority before, not on this scale, not even in Paris.

Then finally I saw another black guy. He wasn't even close – he was 200 metres or so away, in the distance. But I ran to him and introduced myself. He said he was Kenyan, an engineering student. I convinced him to go to a pub. I don't know how, but I convinced him.

The first pub we saw was Irish. He said, 'We can't go in there.'

I said, 'Mate, this is 2003, we can go anywhere.'

He didn't believe me, but he relented: 'Okay, if you walk in first, I'll go right behind you.'

I went up to the ginger-haired, blue-eyed barman and said, 'Can I have a couple of pints of beer, please?' and he responded, 'Coming right up.' Everyone in the room was white, and every-one was looking at us, but I just said to my new Kenyan friend, 'Come on, talk to me.'

We stayed there and talked for a long time. As we left he shook my hand and said, 'I'm very thankful that you did this for me.'

I said, 'I didn't do it for you, I did it for us.'

The next day I went to the beach in Fremantle. It was deserted: there was no one there, which was confusing to me. I wasn't sure if it was safe.

Then a mother and daughter arrived, the girl about four or five. I watched them closely. I was looking at them non-stop, watching everything they were doing. Probably in hindsight that was a bit creepy. I thought, *Whatever they do, I can do*. When they went into the water, I waded in next to them. I said, 'I'm sorry, I'm not from here. I'm not sure if there's sharks around, but I guess if you're swimming here, can I just stay close to you?'

You know, when I think about it now, that would have been very weird for that lady. I was probably about a metre from her; I was really close to her. They would leave the water, and I would leave the water. They would go back into the water, and I would go back into the water. We did this for a while, an odd sort of dance. Then they left the beach, and a few minutes later I left, too.

Melbourne

When I arrived in Melbourne, it was February. By April, I had a job. I remember how easy it was to find one: I was a printer and computer technician, and I got offers from HP, from Epson. I got offers from many multinationals. I was so confused and happy. I came from making a little over $5000 a year, and I got offered $40,000 dollars a year. Soon I had a car and a computer. I could pay my rent, and had enough money to go out for drinks and to the movies.

I finally had dignity.

Steve Bracks was the premier at the time, and Steve Bracks's Victoria had a motto: *Victoria – on the move*. I remember looking at *on the move* on my numberplate, on every numberplate. There was this sense of potential, of promise, like anything was possible. The Premier of Victoria had a Lebanese background. The mayor of Victoria, John So, was Chinese-Australian. I thought, *This is great! I can be anything.*

I lived in St Kilda. My in-laws lived in Toorak. I had to fix printers everywhere, so I was driving all over Melbourne. All you had in those days was the Melways and your memory. To this day, very few of my friends know Melbourne as well as me. I went from Frankston to Sunshine, from Sunshine to Tullamarine, from Tullamarine to Essendon, from Essendon to Moorabbin ... to Boronia ... to Dandenong. It was fantastic: driving around Melbourne, with my tie, with my dignity, with my smile.

I was so eager in my new life that the positives were all I focused on initially. But I remember by about June, I had the thought: *There are no African-diaspora people here*. I was going one or two weeks at a time without seeing another black face. That sense of isolation was really scary.

You want for material things, and then you realise that they mean nothing when you have them without family or friends. You want to share them. You want more.

Then, black people started to show up.

In 2007, my brother migrated to Australia. He was a soccer player, and he even trialled for Adelaide United, but he ended up playing for the Whittlesea Zebras in Victoria's Premier League. At the time there was another black Brazilian playing for the A-League called Leandro Love, and one day the three of us were walking on the street when we met up with AFL player Heritier Lumumba. I owned a fashion boutique by then, and I remember this feeling of four relatively powerful black men walking down the street in Melbourne, shoulder to shoulder. It was incredible.

I thought, *Now I am black, now I am in Australia, now I am an Australian, I can be whoever I want.* I started looking inwards. I started looking to myself and my culture. I began to do my hair in cornrows, after years of shaving to look more 'presentable', to look less black.

One day, Heritier Lumumba took me to Footscray. There were hundreds of black people there! I felt more at home than I had for years.

We went to a black hairdresser's. After decades of getting my hair cut by white people, by Irish and Russian people, I finally got my hair cut by a black man. The way he treated my hair, the way he touched it, was beautiful.

That was the start of my blackness. I had travelled a very long way to find it.

Ravenswood

Grace Williams

Ravenswood was not what I thought Australia would look like. It was stranger and colder than I expected. The polite Christian girl my parents raised me to be would define this suburb of Tasmania, which consisted largely of a sprawling housing commission, as unwelcoming and slightly intimidating. My other, more impolite, self would describe it as a total nightmare.

I arrived in Australia with my family in July 2005. We left Ghana in a rush, and I had no time to say goodbye to my best friend. My parents just whisked the whole family away with no notice. The night before our swift departure, I remember there were a lot of unusual words and acronyms thrown around the one-room tent-slash-hut construction that housed all five of us. One acronym was repeated over and over again: IOM, which stood for International Organization for Migration. Even when I hear it spoken today, it triggers in me uncomfortable memories of confusion and distress. I don't understand why it's still stuck in my head, but other words and phrases from that night stick too, like 'Pretoria' and 'the United Nations'. In adulthood, I have come to understand the meaning and significance of those words, but as a child I found them as foreign as the thought of Ravenswood.

On the day we left Ghana, I felt like a plant in shock, suddenly uprooted from the warm soil that had once held and nurtured me. When I arrived at the airport in Tasmania, it all felt like a dream. We were greeted by white people with signs, standing at the end of a tunnel. It felt like my long journey was finally coming to an end, but even though we had arrived 'home' to Australia, everything felt hostile. Everywhere I turned there seemed to be miles and miles of concrete. Tasmania, a sea of pounded gravel with bright, shock-inducing fluorescent lights, instantly disappointed me. My brother, the latest addition to our family, started to scream. I think there was something about that cold air that disagreed with him, and I couldn't help but feel sympathy.

My family and I were driven to our new house in Launceston's northern suburbs. I looked out the car window, eagerly trying to make out the landscape. From what I had heard about Australia, it was supposed to have miles of beautiful beaches. I was insistent about finding those famed beaches on the way to the house: I kept staring out of the window to see if I could spot some blue in this grey, sluggish landscape, but I found nothing. Instead, the soil here looked strange and rigid. It was odd not to smell the scent of kerosene and mud. This place had no water wells or warmth. There was no familiarity in this landscape; it was nothing like my Ghanaian childhood.

I was born by the sea. My fondest memories of Ghana were of going fishing with my mother. Arriving in Launceston in the winter of 2005 made me feel like someone had told me a great big lie – duped me into believing this place was perfect when it was hell on earth.

The white people gradually thawed and started to become a bit friendlier. They parked outside a strange wooden house that looked like it was falling apart. I wondered if we were going to take a toilet break but, no, they had keys in their hands. It seemed we were going to stay here.

I followed my parents out of the car and into the house. Again, bright lights were flicked on. It seemed like this country had endless amounts of kerosene to waste; lights were being used even in the daytime.

The sky began to dim as we started the tour of our home. I could hear the white people say to my parents, 'This is the kitchen ... That is the bathroom ... This is the lounge,' and then there was a long silence. I stood there staring at my feet. 'That's all for today. If you have any questions we will be in touch,' the woman said. Then a click of the door and finally we were alone, a newly arrived, slightly confused family at home.

I had never been in a wooden house before. My parents always said that wooden houses were poor examples of construction. They didn't like Western homes, because they believed such houses used too much wood and not enough bricks. I wondered why we weren't placed in a brick house. I started to miss my tent-hut in Ghana. At least it was close to the well. All the children played by the well. I suddenly wanted to cry. I missed my friends, but most of all I missed my dog, Champion. I had left her behind without saying a proper goodbye.

Growing up, I noticed that Ravenswood was mostly sad. I never saw joy. No one laughed in the street; no one screamed with delight. The only screams I heard were angry, painful: 'Fuck you!' and then the smashing of glass, followed by more screaming. Crying and fighting and cars burnt out after late-night joy rides marked Ravenswood for me.

I noticed something even stranger in my new homeland: the people looked tattered, poor and unwell. These individuals looked sicker than the friends I had left back in Ghana. In Ravenswood, I saw broken people roaming the streets. Before I had come to Australia, the idea of poor white people was as mythical to me as green fairies in the garden. But this had now become my daily reality. Right in front of me stood poor white people, people who would ask things of me and my family. I saw torn clothes blotched with stains, and a degree of violence and hatred I had never witnessed in the refugee camp in Ghana, but grew to understand as part of the fabric of Ravenswood. The truth is, housing commissions attract the most fascinating types.

Even though I grew up in a developing country, I spoke English well, along with other languages: Mende and Krio, a little bit of French. I could read and write, and I practised my spelling because I had to – we had no autocorrect in West Africa. When I would try to communicate with people in primary school in Tasmania, I was surprised by their sentences and speech patterns, their written language and spelling. I was surprised that the teachers didn't cane students every time they got something wrong.

In Ghana, I read the whole Bible back to front, along with any other text I could get my hands on. I later discovered, in my adult life, that Tasmania has a fifty per cent functional illiteracy rate. This is not what I expected from a 'developed' and wealthy nation such as Australia. When I arrived in Tasmania as an eight-year-old I was probably further ahead of half the adult population in terms of literacy.

But I still had a language barrier. Idioms and expressions were something I had to learn in the schoolyard.

I have a vivid memory of getting into a spat in primary school. My best friend at the time, a girl whose name I cannot remember, asked if I was mad at her. I was deeply offended by this statement. I looked at her gloweringly when she kept repeating it.

'Grace, are you mad at me?' she said, over and over.

I finally gave up on the silent treatment and replied, 'Are you implying that I need to be placed in a mental hospital because I am a mad person?'

She looked at me, confused. 'What?'

'That's what you mean when you say "mad" – mentally sick, unwell, mad! Well, I am not mad at all.'

I don't think my friend understood what I was trying to say. I must have looked really funny, getting upset and interpreting those words in a context she had never considered. Later, as I got to know Australian slang, I discovered that 'mad' is a synonym for 'angry'. I was never angry at my friend; I was just being my introverted self.

I encountered a map of Tasmania later in primary school. I finally realised why there was no beach around me. I was in the Tamar Valley. I now understood that I was on an island, which didn't really seem to be part of Australia. Everyone in Ravenswood – in fact, everyone in Tasmania – called the rest of Australia 'the mainland', and now I could see why.

On the map, the mainland looked so huge and forbidding that I started to prefer Tasmania. Tasmania was small and manageable. It didn't seem as though I could ever get lost on this island; it was so compact in comparison to everything else. Near Ravenswood, there was a place called Cataract Gorge. My first time in a swimming pool was at the gorge, with about 500 other people, in the heat of a midsummer Tasmanian day. The pool was bright blue. All the people around me had such glaringly pale skin, it looked as though they were sheets of paper that reflected the sun, and then slowly turned to red as the day continued.

The pool was an artificial replacement for the sea I yearned for. The first time I visited Tasmania's coastline, it was glorious. I swam at Greens Beach, jumping up and down in the monster waves. I finally felt like I had come home. This was like the West African coastline I remembered, and even though the water felt colder, it still embraced me.

After finding home in Australia at the seaside, I remember the day that new home was challenged. The day a glass bottle was thrown at me from a moving car. The day someone screamed the unexpected 'Go back to your country.' The day that phrase became recurring, when two boys in my high school cornered me behind the lockers in an attempt to intimidate me, chanting the familiar phrase of the powerless and insecure, 'Go back to your country,' hissing like snakes.

I remember walking into Coles supermarket with my mother and having a shop assistant ask me, 'Aren't you grateful that Australia took you in?' I was surprised when my mother leapt into the conversation to rescue me by educating this woman about some key factors of the refugee existence. My mother, in a gentle voice I had never heard before, corrected her with grace. Under the fluorescent lights, I heard her say, 'My country is wonderful, and I miss it very much. If it wasn't for war we wouldn't be here. This is not a choice we willingly made.' The truth is, Australia chose us, not the other way around.

The myth of Australia's heroism and kindness towards poor refugees blinds many white middle-class Australians from the realities of tents of homeless in the city streets, and housing commission communities in the suburbs, like Ravenswood. Many are blinded, too, to the suffering of Indigenous peoples, who still live like exiles in their own land.

The day Australia truly became my home was when all my links to Ghana died.

As I am a child of refugee parents, living in a camp was a reality of my life for a time. This reality wasn't too bad. My first memories were of sleeping in a bed with my parents and my dog, Champion.

People in camps inevitably leave, and the friends you grow

up with end up in unknown places. All that is left of them are fading memories.

One day we heard some terrible news from people we knew in the camp who were still awaiting resettlement. Champion had been murdered by a group of people who craved meat. I left our house and walked outside, away from my family, too embarrassed to cry in front of them. At eleven years old, I wiped my tears quietly, avoiding making a fuss about something so trivial. It was in that moment, when I heard of her death, that I realised all my ties to Ghana were now cut.

Recently, I was painting a plain white box as part of a street-art project in Hobart. I was with a friend, Annie, a white woman who had recently moved to Tasmania. As we were working on the painting, a man came close to me and asked, 'Where are you from?'

I responded by asking him another question. 'Are you trying to ask me why I'm black and in Tasmania?'

There was a long pause before Annie interjected. 'Mate, I'm from New Zealand. Why aren't you asking me where I'm from? She's more Australian than me.'

I have come to learn that whiteness does not equal Australian-ness. My home has become a little island that often gets short shrift on tourist key rings of the map of Australia. I have come to learn that there is no need to justify my presence in my home. After all, the roots of this nation belong to black First Nations peoples. I am as Australian as anyone whose family has come to this island from across the seas.

Both

Vulindlela Mkwananzi

One of my first memories as a child is shaking Nelson Mandela's hand, in a church in Ashfield, New South Wales. I was three years old. The reason I remember this so well is because he only patted my twin brother on the head, so I was flush with the glory of the handshake. We laugh about it now.

I knew that Mandela was important because he was sur-rounded by lots of people making a fuss. We had recently moved from Zimbabwe, which at that age I thought was called Zim-bye-bye, because that's what everyone was saying to us the day we left. My mother, my father, my twin brother and I never returned to Zimbabwe all together again.

My father was a printer in Zimbabwe, born there and raised by his Gogo (Gogo means 'grandmother' in Ndebele, my father's language). He met my Australian mother there, while she was travelling round the country.

It wasn't until I grew older that I started to ponder how contro-versial it was for both of my parents' families to have mixed-race grandchildren, for different reasons. It certainly wasn't fashion-able at that time; it was a serious life choice that had meaningful consequences.

For my family in Zimbabwe, it meant that my brother and I might grow up not knowing our culture – we might not be raised the 'African' way. For my mother's family in New South Wales, it was a shock to have 'coloured' children, a point of shame and a source of exclusion from a conservative white community that prided itself on its sense of 'Australianness'. I can't say for sure, but I believe this is the reason, coupled with the trauma of the loss of my mother, that I know so little about my mother's family to this day.

Both of my parents died in a car accident when I was three. After much controversy about who would raise us, including, I'm told, the possibility of being adopted by an affluent Jewish family on the northern shores of Sydney, my twin brother and I were given to my stepmum, my birth mother's best friend.

I call her Mum to this day. I can't express in words how thankful I am that her family took us in, as they truly are very special people to my brother and me.

Growing up African-Australian, especially in our particularly unique circumstances, shaped the way I am today.

My parents were activists: my father actively fought apartheid in South Africa from Zimbabwe, and my mother was a women's liberation campaigner. My upbringing was very much informed by politics, from attending rallies to seeing political posters to hosting exiled African National Congress members in the squat we lived in, in Erskineville. Throughout my life I have been fortunate to stay in touch with my family in Zimbabwe, visiting them every few years. The visits are always fleeting, powerful and heartbreaking all at the same time.

Growing up in Australia with a mix of these two identities, Zimbabwean and Australian, is hard to explain: there are so many different angles from which I look at it. I think about it a lot. Every day, to be honest.

When I go to Zimbabwe, I realise how divorced from my culture I am – how much that one tragic event of my father's death has denied me an education and a body of experiences that I can only imagine now. I am so hungry to learn about my culture that I write things down and ask many questions, but it's never enough. I know that my thirst for knowledge, and desire to understand my parents, will never be quenched.

In Australia, it's quite different. I have pieced together a lot about my mother from hearing my stepmother's descriptions and anecdotes, from brief encounters with her friends, and in between the strange awkward silences in the rare moments I interact with my blood relatives.

It didn't take me long as a child to realise that being brown was going to affect my life. My strongest memory, stronger even than meeting Mandela, was from primary school, when a kid called me a 'nigger'. I knew what it meant, and in a panic to launch a comeback, I thought of the first thing that popped into my head that was white – a peeled banana. It didn't have the same impact, and that shook me instantly. I think that's why I remember it so distinctly. *Why isn't there an equivalent word for 'nigger' that is as cutting and as powerful?* I wondered.

My stepmother exposed me to certain films and ideas, from movies of Steve Biko to Bryce Courtenay's *The Power of One* to stories of the Soweto Massacre. It always puzzled me in these films, books and documentaries that skin colour was such an incredibly big deal, considering I was both black and white, and didn't feel either side dictated anything much about my personality. Skin colour seemed so absurdly arbitrary, but it was clear that at some point in history certain groups had decided it was reason enough to divide and attack one another.

I always find strange the terms that people with parents from two different cultural backgrounds are called: half-caste, mixed-race, coloured. Why do I have to be *half*? Why *caste*? Why *mixed*? I am *both*: it is what makes me who I am, and in my romanticised moments, I see my birth as proof that love conquers division.

In my most cynical moments, I wonder if my mother fetishised my father as a black man, or if marriage to my mother was my father's attempt to escape the situation in Zimbabwe, after he'd seen the number of wealthy white people continually passing through there. Honestly, to me it doesn't matter at all, but perhaps if I had been able to know my parents more, I would have understood their relationship in greater depth. Perhaps those cynical ideas are far off the mark. Perhaps they are completely true.

It took me a long time to realise that my stepmother had no idea of some of my brother's and my experiences in growing up as African-Australians. Once, we went to the shops and (as would often happen) the shopkeeper followed us, thinking we were going to steal something. My stepmother saw this, and asked the shopkeeper what on earth he was doing. We laughed, and told her to calm down. 'It happens all the time, Mum,' we said. Now, when my stepmother tells me this story, her eyes well up a little, and I realise her pain in her powerlessness to protect us from what our physical appearance means in Australia. It also makes me realise that she can have all the compassion in the world, but still never quite understand what it means, and what it really feels like, to be in our skin here.

I recall my first time returning to Zimbabwe, at age nine, and thinking to myself, *Oh, wow, it's gonna be great – there's no discrimination there.* Instead, our light skin was pointed out and remarked upon, with people asking us why we had African names but were so white. I began to comprehend the strange position of being from two distinctly different cultures – that there is literally nowhere on the planet where the majority of people look like you.

The most revealing thing about this is that it has made me see the power of psychological homogeneity, and the beauty in its unifying power and the sense of belonging it can give, as well as the incredible divisive power it has.

I believe most truths are often paradoxical: they have both a dark and a light side, and sometimes even more than two sides.

At the same time, people are not homogeneous at all, and even if the entire planet was African-Australian like me, humans would find another reason to create a division based on physical appearance. The same discrimination would just take on a different form.

I couldn't tell you what it is like to be African-Australian, as I don't know what it is like not to be – I have no external point of reference for my experiences, just like everyone else. This is why people's individual stories are so important. I think my own experiences have greatly informed the lens I see the world through, and I like to share my story with others.

It's so clear to me now that there are power imbalances that have existed for so long that need to shift. They are so ingrained in cultures, and so buried, that it takes a lot of digging, very deep, to excavate the truth.

My stepmother told me a quote my mother once wrote, and it has resonated with me deeply.

Men must release power,
And women must seize it,
And throw it to the winds – its rightful place.

This, to me, holds true not just for gender imbalance but also for racial imbalance, economic imbalance and all systemic power structures that we have built.

When I think of how I see the world now, growing up African in Australia, and my early memory of shaking Nelson Mandela's hand, something inside of me stirs, and I feel driven to strive for change.

Di Apprentice

Tinashe Pwiti

Kuda and I were twins. We had the typical sibling relationship: we bickered a lot, yet were very close. Kuda was the only boy in our family, so he was pretty spoilt. He was the golden child, and he knew it.

We were born in Harare, the capital of Zimbabwe. Kuda and I lived with our parents and our two older sisters.

We both came to Australia in 2008. At the time, the situation in Zimbabwe wasn't great. It still isn't much better. There was a lack of jobs and limited opportunities for education. My parents decided that they would pack their twins off to Australia to get an education and, hopefully after that, a job. They were also considering other countries, including the United States or Britain, but we had a distant cousin here, and I think my parents just thought, *Well, we might as well send them there.* So in some ways, Australia chose us.

Other than boarding school, Australia was the first time we'd been away from home. Just before we boarded the plane from Harare, Kuda extended his palm out to me and grabbed my hand. We got on the plane holding hands. He didn't have to say anything. It was his way of telling me, *We're in this together. It's just you and me now.*

We were adults, but still young. As an immigrant, you grow up fast, I guess. You're forced to grow up. Being my only brother, Kuda felt like it was his responsibility as a man, I think, to look after me in Australia, but he failed miserably at that. I think women mature faster, and after we arrived here, I mothered him a lot – consciously or not. It was an interesting shift in our dynamic.

For the first few months, we stuck to the familiar. We found the local Zimbabwean community. Then we ventured outside of that and made friends elsewhere. I lived in share-house accommodation with an Australian couple. I found them really welcoming. They were used to letting out their room to students, and it was a nice environment.

I was living in Moorabbin, and Kuda was living in Chadstone, and we didn't have cars, so we had to figure out how to see each other – navigating the public transport system and all that. We developed an arrangement where I would visit him every Sunday.

My studies were tough. I mean, study was what we had come here for, but it was tough. I had enrolled in hospitality, and Kuda was studying information technology. I enjoyed my course, though, and did well. My brother, not so much. He became distracted by other things. Six months after we arrived, he dropped out. Until then it seemed as though Kuda had adjusted well to the move, but I guess, in hindsight, maybe he hadn't. He started partying. There were girls and other things.

For a while, my parents didn't know he'd dropped out.

A year into our being in Australia, Kuda started his music career. First he began performing in a hip-hop band; he knew one of the guys in the band from high school back in Zimbabwe. They were just boys mucking around in a garage, rapping, and then Kuda realised he loved what he was doing, and was actually talented at it. He started performing reggae and dancehall. He did well at it: he was getting instrumental gigs from producers, and he soon became a dancehall and reggae singer. It's not something he had been especially interested in back home. We loved that kind of music, growing up, but I don't think either of us ever thought he was going to be an artist. Coming to Australia gave him the space to explore that. He definitely had more opportunities here. He got them, and he ran with them.

Kuda met his girlfriend, Catherine, who later became his wife, about two years after we arrived. She taught dancehall, so she kind of helped him with the music. She had some connections here with DJs and producers.

By this stage, my parents knew that Kuda had dropped out of his course and was working. They thought he was doing the music thing on the side of a day job. I don't think they realised how much his music career had kicked off.

His gigs were amazing. I remember the first time I heard him perform: it was around November 2011, and the event was a white party on a cruise ship. It was pretty incredible. I was blown away, because this was just my stupid twin brother – that's how I saw him. But onstage, he was a charismatic artist with so much energy. The crowd loved him.

Mostly, though, he'd play in grungy bars and pubs. The typical reggae club here is not that big – it's not a genre that's well known in Australia, though it is picking up a bit now.

Studies got easier for me. I started working at a restaurant as well, and once I was in the industry, I could see what all the academic learning was about. I enjoyed it, even though working in a kitchen was hard. I still enjoy it, and I'm a chef now.

While Kuda was doing his music, he also had other work, when he could find it. He'd go from job to job. He did your typical forklift labour type of thing; he did a bit of landscaping. It was never very stable, and he wasn't very focused. I think he found it hard to find work because he didn't have qualifications. For a decent chunk of time, he wasn't working.

I fell pregnant with my then partner towards the end of my course, and I had a son. Then Catherine and Kuda got married and had a child. Our kids are a year apart.

Motherhood was a shock. I was only twenty-two when I fell pregnant. It wasn't part of the plan, but it happened.

When I fell pregnant, my mother was keen for me and Kuda to come home. She probably thought, *They're both young, they're there on their own, what do they know?* But we managed to convince her that we were doing reasonably okay, which we were.

We tried to support each other, Kuda and I. We knew we were both young to be parents. We were in a serious relationship or marriage when we were far too young for it, but I guess we were still mature enough to realise that we should support each other the best we could. It was challenging. Here, without much family, you're on your own. There's daycare and all that, but it's expensive. I was also in an abusive relationship.

I was fortunate to be close to Catherine as well. We were there for each other. Seeing our kids play together was lovely. They were both boys, and they got on well. They still do.

Kuda wasn't ready to be a father. They say kids change you, that once you have a child you have to step up. I did. I had my kid before him, and I was forced to grow up very quickly. Given the relationship I was in, it wasn't easy, but when I realised I was going to raise my child here, it hit me: *I'm away from home. I'm a young mum. This is my life here, in Australia.* I'd been here long enough to call it home by then, but there's something about having a child that cements that. *My child's first memories will be here*, I remember thinking. I've thought more about that as my son gets older, what with finding him a school. You become part of a community.

Not Kuda. He didn't step up to the plate at all.

Kuda didn't handle marriage or fatherhood well. He began to take drugs. I think it started with the music scene, unfortunately: drugs are part of the lifestyle, and that's where he picked up the habit. When we were growing up in Zimbabwe, there was not a lot of drugs. There was marijuana, but not hard drugs. I'd never experienced drug-taking in my life. I didn't even know what someone looked like when they were high. The first time I became aware of Kuda's drug use was when he came to visit me after I had given birth to my son. He went into a room and came out some time later. I remember going in afterwards, and there was this white powder on the table. I saw it, and I just thought *What is that?* It still didn't register, because I hadn't ever been exposed to it. I just cleaned it up.

Drugs took hold of him, and wouldn't let go. They completely changed him. He became a narcissist. He became arrogant. That's not who he was. Soon his marriage was on the rocks, and he wasn't working. I was having to relay all this back to Mum. I told her, 'Things are serious. It's beyond me. It's beyond his wife. You're the parent – will you please come and try to sort this out?'

Neither of us had been back home at that point. Still now I haven't been back. It's expensive. My parents are pretty well off, though. She finally came here, my mum. Unfortunately, she was in denial. He, the only boy in the family, could do no wrong, and she wouldn't accept that her golden child was in trouble. I was saying 'there is a problem', and his wife was saying 'there is a problem', and it was obvious there was, but she didn't want to see it.

Kuda was denying the severity of his addiction. He was saying he did drugs occasionally, recreationally, and it was under control. He was saying what your typical addict says. My mum bought into that, unfortunately. She had it in her mind that the problem was the marriage.

We're in this together. It's you and me now. That's what I felt he'd meant as he took my hand and we got on the plane to Australia together. But I'd lost that Kuda. I lost him once the drugs took hold. I used to say to him, 'I want that guy back. That guy who held my hand on the plane – that's the guy that I'm looking for.'

Onstage, he began to put on this gangster macho persona, and he went by the name Di Apprentice. It was hard to tell what was the stage persona and what was the drugs. It was hard to tell who was Kuda and who was Di Apprentice; they'd kind of mesh together. It was sad to see this twin, this brother I grew up with, who was in the same womb as me, become someone I didn't recognise anymore.

Kuda had gone to a privileged boys' high school back in Zimbabwe. He'd hinted to me that he'd been bullied there and my parents didn't do anything about it. Looking back now, I see that as a kid, he was small. He was not timid, exactly, but the jocks of the school would have identified him as a loser, and he unfortunately felt that way about himself. There was always this element of trying to please the tough kids, and when we came here, the guys he was hanging out with in the drug scene would have been the same tough kids he was trying to prove himself to back in high school. He still wanted approval from the cool kids. And as he became this big artist and lived a party lifestyle, it was like he'd made it.

Then the suicide attempts started. The first one was in 2014, just after I had my second child. She was maybe a month old. I went to visit Kuda and his family on a Sunday. He'd just had a fight with Catherine. He grabbed some knives from the kitchen and locked himself in the bathroom. Catherine said to me, 'This is not the first time this has happened. He's done it before.' We decided to call the police and let them handle it. With each of his attempts, that's what we did: we let the police handle it. That's all we could do. Having to call the police on your twin brother or your husband – can you imagine it?

He wasn't high at the time, but we let the police know that he had been using ice, and they were aware that one of the side effects of ice is suicidal ideation. They managed to calm him down. They got him out of the bathroom, and they handcuffed him and took him off to hospital. We were standing on the footpath, watching this. I remember the look on his face. He wasn't aggressive; he was never aggressive towards us, only towards himself. It was like he was thinking, *When did this become my life? Why am I on the ground, a black man, being handcuffed?*

We didn't know then how bad ice was. It wasn't until a bit later, when we started hearing about it on the news, or reading about it in the paper, that we realised how serious it was. That was the start of the ice epidemic in Australia, but we saw the effects firsthand, up close.

Threats of self-harm happened regularly after that first incident I witnessed. If I were to count how many times, I would run out of fingers. After every attempt, I would ring my parents and say, 'There's been another attempt. This is happening again.' It was always after fights with Catherine. He was still denying that he was on drugs. He would get caught cheating, too, and deny that. The threats of self-harm were about him losing control of a situation and then wanting to take hold of it again as much as he could. It was as though he felt that threatening suicide was the ultimate way to gain control. Everyone came running. We did, because you can't not.

In all those early attempts, I don't think he intended to die, because of the methods he used. He would get what he wanted. He would get people to come running. As a sober person, you could see what was going on, but you could not ignore it. It was too risky. Catherine and I had to respond accordingly.

The biggest disappointment was my parents' reaction. They didn't understand the severity of the situation because they weren't here. It was like they thought, *We sent you there together, you deal with it. Just look after him.*

I don't blame them, but I've had to make peace with their decisions.

Finally, Catherine and I managed to make my parents take the situation seriously. They were going to bring Kuda back to Zimbabwe and put him in rehab. That was a relief, but it was also sad. Kuda and I always used to say to one another, 'We came here together, into this world and from Zimbabwe, and when we go back, we will go together.'

He didn't want to leave. He knew he was going back for a bit of a break, but he didn't know he was going into rehab. He was married, but didn't have his residency here, because he hadn't sorted it out. He was worried that if he went to Zimbabwe, he would not be allowed to return. Yet at the same time, I think he recognised there was no other option.

A couple of days before he was supposed to leave, I rang him to have a chat, and he was in a very bad place. He and Catherine had a studio in Brunswick. I arranged to see him at the studio.

The second I walked through the door, he started picking a fight with Catherine. I said, 'Come on, let's you and I just go to your studio booth.' I remember the last thing he said to Catherine was 'Fine. You want me gone? I'm gone.'

He used to record in his studio booth. Sometimes he used to take the handle off the door so people couldn't interrupt him while he was recording. I saw him do that, and I didn't think anything of it. I said, 'I'll come back and see you tomorrow. You're worked up now. I'll talk to you then. I love you.'

He replied, 'I love you.'

I said, 'Can I give you a hug?'

He said, 'No, it's okay. I can feel your love from here.' He closed the door.

Catherine called me at about 9.00 am the next day and said, 'From the time you left the studio until this morning, I've been here, and he hasn't come out. I've just left the studio and his car's still there. I'm worried.'

We rang the police, and my partner met them at the studio with keys. He called soon after and said, 'He's gone. He hung himself.'

Catherine broke down. I went into shock. I didn't believe it. I said, 'Put the police on the phone.' A police officer got on the phone, and he said, 'Yes, we're sorry, it's true.'

....

The biggest lesson that has emerged from this loss for me is the importance of talking about mental health, suicide and drug addiction. Kuda was suffering from drug-induced depression. He'd been seeing a counsellor prior to his death, who had diagnosed him with borderline personality disorder. We didn't even find this out until afterwards.

The stigma attached to mental-health issues and suicide is so significant. This needs to change. These sorts of things are happening every day, and we need to talk about them without feeling ashamed or scared. Kuda didn't speak up. The drug use was probably his means of escape, instead of talking about things. Kuda also ticked all the boxes for not being able to get help, because he wasn't a resident, he was too old for a lot of services, and he was too young for others. He fell through the gaps in terms of both mental-health and drug-addiction services. It was devastating. I think there was only one residential rehab place we rang here that would have been able to take him, and it was just too expensive.

I was in an abusive relationship with my son's father, but I was able to get help. I've been able to get counselling and support. I also spoke up. I was willing to talk about the fact that I was struggling, and ask for the help that I needed.

We did some research into borderline personality disorder after we found out that Kuda had been diagnosed with it, and in hindsight it all makes sense – that whole dynamic between Kuda, and Di Apprentice, and the father, and the friend, and the brother ... I look back now, and I see the different characters he was, and it just fits into place.

Grief is my constant visitor. I lie down with it at night, and I wake up with it in the morning. It's always there, but I'm not afraid of it anymore. I've learnt to live alongside it. We should talk about this terrible thing that happens, grief, more often. It's forever. It's worthy of being talked about.

Families are left behind. A kid is without his father right now because of stigma and silence and shame. Still, to this day, I can't sit down and talk to my parents about my brother's death. They are of a certain generation and culture where this topic is out of bounds.

I'm not even sure if I should identify as a twin anymore. I had a twin, and now he's gone. I miss Kuda so much. There is not a day that goes by, not a moment, that I am not thinking about him. Not one single moment.

I remember once, as kids, we went on holiday somewhere, and my father stupidly got one gift from a store for Kuda and me. One gift, to share between twins! I think it was one of those squishy souvenir balls or something. We fought and fought over it, until my father said, 'If you can't share it, nobody gets it.' We looked at each other, and we decided to rip the toy in half, so we each had a piece.

Two pieces, but no whole anymore.

My Family Abroad

Adut Wol Akec

My Family Abroad

My family abroad live on an island surrounded by water.

My father once called it a prison on water where everyone must pay to live, must pay to breathe and must be reminded every day of how lucky they are.

My family abroad live in luxury, the only kind of luxury you live when you have come from nothing.

My family abroad left a country in war, left their houses, their loved ones, and took with them what they could carry.

A handful of kids.

My family abroad are still attached to my family at home, all attached by a telephone call.

My family abroad use their telephone privileges supplied by Centrelink of ten dollars a day to hear the crackling and static of our family at home.

A successful day for my family abroad is when after yelling and screaming, 'HELLO, HELLO, it is network, can you hear me?' we get, 'HELLO is that you, it is so wonderful to hear from you again.'

'HELLO, HELLO, we are doing fine.'

'HOW is everyone?'

'Everyone is sick, the old weep and creak with every century added to the bone, the young weep with every century added to … to … Everyone is weak.'

'The government will pay me in a week. I will send help, my family at home.'

My family abroad skip another overdue bill.

'Put it up there, right on top of the other overdue bills, I will pay it next Centrelink pay.'

Up on top of the water bill, up on top of the electricity bill, up on top of the housing bill.

My family abroad are attached to the government
like a child to a tit.

My Aunty Poor

My aunty poor works in a cold freezer.

She works to feed her sister at home, her daughter
in her room, a son at the gym.

My aunty poor has never known poverty, never seen it,
felt it or tasted it.

She lives in the memories of the wealth she had as a girl.

My aunty works hard; she works harder than the fleeting memories of wealth back on the farm

Back in the village

Back home

Back in her mind.

My aunty works hard, the bills work harder.

Illness at home worker.

My aunty worked so hard, fought illnesses abroad.

She developed a tumour in her ear that was caused by allergies.

She brushed it off: what are allergies to malaria?

Her sister's husband's daughter has malaria.

My aunty had surgery to remove her tumour. Lost a bit of eyesight too.

Nevertheless, my aunty works hard.

She went back to the same job because bills on top of bills, on top of bills.

My aunty poor abroad cannot see poverty even if it hit her in the face and left her blind in one eye.

My aunty poor cannot see poverty because she has a job.

My Mother Arranged

My mother was more surprised to find herself mothering
and fathering seven kids by herself after thirteen years
abroad.

She was more surprised about that than the day
she found out she was to marry a Dinka man.

My mother arranged telephone calls to our father
at home. He tried to father us over the telephone.

She arranged for a roof over our heads

Food on our table

English on our tongues

My mother arranged for work with no English.

Our arranged mother spoke to us in our father's
language.

For ten years, our mother arranged for us to learn
two different languages while she forgot her own.

My mother arranged parent–teacher interviews, only
to have us translate what they said to her and what she
wanted to say to them.

My mother arranged, arranged for her seven kids to go
to school, while knowing no English. We read to her
school forms and letters, and even arranged her signature
when needed.

My mother arranged, she arranged for her life to revolve around her husband, her children and her time.

My Telephone Dad

My telephone dad likes to remind me he is my father.

I linked his voice to his words to his breath.

My telephone dad thinks yelling at me on the phone works.

My telephone dad tells our arranged mum how to raise us

How to keep us in order

What he wants us to know

To learn

To study

To marry.

My telephone dad is funny.

He is funny because even though he knows I could choose to not listen to him – after all, he is just on the phone – he puts his base over the phone to scare us, as if we should know he put his foot down.

He likes to remind us of how much he sacrificed by sending us abroad

How hard he had to work to pay for us.

All that while on the phone.

My telephone dad wanted a doctor, he got a failing scientist who only passed by a prayer.

My telephone dad wanted a doctor, he got a nurse.

He wanted a lawyer, he got a therapist.

Wanted a successor to his name.

Got resentment from his son.

My telephone dad does not understand how his sons do not know him.

Why his sons do not know what it takes to be a man of the house.

After all, he did tell them over the phone.

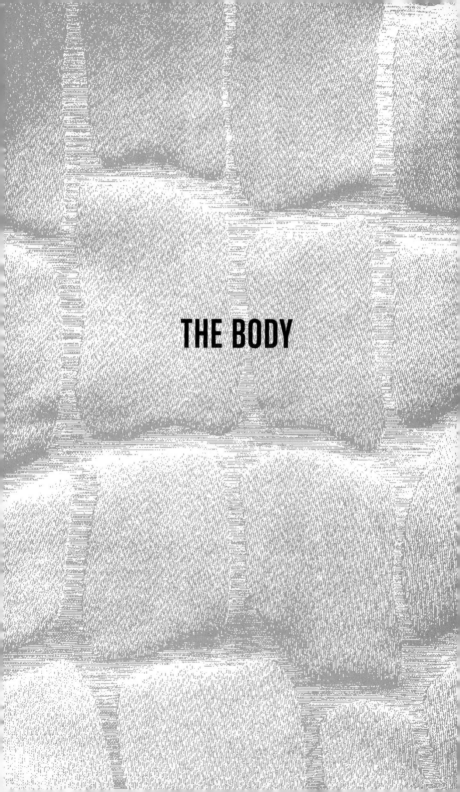

THE BODY

Ashy Knees

Manal Younus

'Don't kneel
or crawl
or your knees will go black.'

She was taught to hate her ashy knees
see they were black
and black was bad
but she was black.
      'Don't call yourself black;
      you're brown,'
she'd hear
as though that should make her feel better
but still not even the black boys would look at her

so she wanted
her lips to be as thin as the other girls
her hips as slim as the other girls
but with fingertips that didn't match her knuckles.

She was the scapegoat for lies
the victim of exclusion
should she be here or there
until she came to the conclusion
that she didn't belong anywhere.

Introduced as 'Sarah's little black friend'.

    'What's your name again?'

    'Can I just call you Mia then?'

Skin tone meant
we got teased in the schoolyard
she pretended to be tough
but they would call her bluff
when pushed
she landed on those knees

making them darker
ashier
her
angrier.

In the afro hair houses
scalp burning with hydrochloride
I'd wander down aisles
while trying to find something to scrub off parts of
   this child
these
ashy knees needed creams
these nappy locks should be stopped
this rainbow of browns looked down on.

And why
was I praised for having such white palms
these arms
change by sunlight

    'So stay out of the sun,'
I'd hear.

    'You're getting too dark.'
Such simple words enough to spark a disdain
for this blackness.
'Or you'll look like a slave.'
As though slavery was a bad choice our ancestors made.

She said, 'You're not even black
    just tanned
    you've got skin we'd kill for.'

Well, tell that to those who got killed for it
police-stopped,
    billed for it
skin peeled from toxins never healed from it
parents stolen from grandparents
land grabs,
    displacement
derogated,
    shamed
second-class citizens
    on our own lands
      that you claim.

If only it was as simple as colour
or varying body types
but for generations
these would determine our fates
and they still do in so many places
still threatened by our faces

so we get pulled apart
and they take what they feel like taking
black lips
black curves
black hair
       skin
       language
       culture
       land.

But all these parts
make a whole soul
that knows no notion of giving in
we will hold ourselves together.

This team light
team dark skin
means we divide us
but on what basis
when even the palest
can come from the blackest dust

just by uniting
just by existing
we not only resist
we define resistance.

See, I was taught to hate
these ashy knees
but there's so much they tell
the stories

of those times even I
tried to rid me of me
but didn't succeed

thank you
ashy knees

African Mama

Sara El Sayed

'We always want what we don't have,' my mother said, on our first visit to African Mama. Straight hair being what we both didn't have.

My neck was cramped from leaning onto the basin, cold and wet, and my scalp burnt from the Dark and Lovely chemical hair straightener that had been left on a bit too long. I tried to distract myself by counting the braids on the women in the posters adorning the purple walls.

'I think it's enough now,' I said to my mother, as I gave up my stoicism and stared at the ceiling through wincing eyes.

'Just a little longer, or you won't notice a difference,' she said from the chair beside me. I wondered how much she was feeling it.

The hairdresser, Mary, returned and turned on the shower-head. I saw my mother shuffle in her chair as she waited for her turn.

'Water okay?' Mary's words gurgled through the stream running down my ears.

I nodded. It was uncomfortably cold, but this was needed to relieve my burning scalp. I felt lighter as I sat up, water dripping down my back. Shuffling over to my seat at the mirror, I heard my mother let out a sigh of relief as Mary turned on the other showerhead.

My hair was flat. Its usual kinks were gone, replaced by limp strands. I was happy. I reached for my hot tea and sipped slowly.

'Samuel!' Mary called.

'Yes?'

Mary's Ghanaian accent contrasted with her son's Australian response. 'Bring the product, please.'

Samuel, who couldn't have been more than two years older than me, placed a large tub of product on the bench, took some in his hands and dispersed it throughout my wet hair. 'So you and your mum are from Egypt?'

'Yes. So, Africa, but not *Africa* Africa.'

'*Africa* Africa?'

'You know – North Africa, not South Africa.' *Brown Africa, not black Africa.*

'We're from West Africa. Still Africa.' He saw redness on my scalp. 'That Dark and Lovely stuff looks like it burns,' he said.

'Yeah. But I hope it will make me look "lovely".' I smiled.

'Red and lovely. Not dark, though!' He laughed.

Mary approached and Samuel returned to the front counter. My hair danced around her hands and into the air and she blow-dried it. 'So lovely!' she yelled over the noise.

....

Several years later, I sat in the chair at Shine Salon. It truly was shiny, from the glossy benches to the gleaming women in the posters on the white walls.

I untied my hair and watched the hairdresser's face grow in concern.

'It's so curly!' she said, trying to comb her fingers through it. The more she did this, the bigger my hair became. 'Like an afro!'

I fought the urge to argue. *It's not an afro. Not everything that's not pin straight is an afro. Not everything that doesn't look like your posters is an afro.*

'Looks a bit like dreads when it's down like this.'

I bit my tongue. 'It can be a handful,' I said.

'Would you like a drink or a magazine before we get started?'

'No, thank you, I'm fine.' I smiled.

'So, where are you from? Where did you get this interesting hair from?' She curled a strand around her finger and then tried to pull it free. It didn't uncoil as easily as she'd thought.

'Egypt.'

'Wow! Must be a lot different living here though, huh?'

'Oh yeah – but I've been in Australia since I was seven, so sixteen years has been enough time to get used to it.'

'Must be so hot there.'

'Sometimes. Here's hot too.'

She smiled. 'True. How do you wear it?'

'Up.'

'Always?'

'Most of the time. Unless I straighten it. It looks too messy otherwise.'

'You shouldn't tie it up so much. You've got a lot of breakage where your hairtie sits.' She lifted a hand mirror to show me the breakage at the back of my head. 'Try wearing it down more.'

'Okay.' I had no intention of wearing it down more.

'So, what are we doing today?'

'Just an iron straighten, please.'

'Do you want to add a treatment?' The treatment she was talking about, which I had tried before, did as much for my hair as a declawed cat scratching a curtain.

'No thanks – they don't really work for me.'

'Oh, but they're great! They'll make your hair much, much softer and will make the straighten last much, much longer.'

'I've tried them before. They sound great, just not for me.'

'Trust me, I know a lot of people with your type of hair and it works for them.'

I am a person with my type of hair.

After the wash, the blow-dry revealed what I had been delaying telling the hairdresser.

'Do you do anything else to your hair other than iron straighten? Do you colour it?'

'No, I don't colour it.'

She fingered a strand that kinked at the roots but went straight near the ends. Like a heartline going flat. 'It's all basically dead,' she said.

'It looks like that because I get it chemically straightened sometimes.'

Sometimes.

What ensued was a lecture that I had heard from many hairdressers before. Using such harsh chemicals on my hair ruins it. I'm irreparably damaging my hair. The chemicals I'm using are most likely wrong for me. The salon's products are so much better.

And, my favourite: I should learn to love my hair the way it is, naturally.

'I know. But I've done it since I was twelve years old, and it helps me manage it.'

She clutched her chest. 'Twelve?! I'm surprised all your hair hasn't fallen out by now! Please tell me you don't do it yourself.'

'No,' I said, although sometimes I did, 'I go to a place called African Mama.'

'Their products are probably made especially for African hair, not for yours.'

I hesitated for a moment. 'Well, I am African.'

'You know what I mean,' she said.

Complex Colour

Carly Findlay

When I was little, I wanted to have 'normal' skin. I would often pull up my sleeves and look at my forearms, showing them off to the kids at school. These kids weren't really my friends – I didn't have many.

My arms were the part of my body that could pass as 'normal'.

I grew up in Walla Walla, a tiny country town in New South Wales, close to the Victorian border. The summers were scorching hot and dry; the winters, frosty. It was a farming community – sheep and cattle were raised for slaughter, and wheat would be harvested yearly. I wondered how many rats lived in the grain silos. Most people were white and Christian. My parents worked in a small rural city thirty minutes from home – which was different from the parents of my peers, who all seemed to work on the land or within Walla Walla. We lived in a tiny weatherboard house on half an acre. Our garden was abundant with vegetables and sunflowers, and our dogs ran happily in the yard.

If I were to wear a mask and long pants and just bare my forearms, I could pretend I didn't have ichthyosis – the rare, severe and painful congenital condition that makes my skin red and scaly. The skin on my forearms is, most of the time, smooth and pale. It only gets red when I'm sore. I used to ask the kids at school whether I would be white or black or brown if I didn't have red skin. 'White!' they would say, nodding their heads furiously. White, like it was the desired, socially acceptable shade. Were they trying to tell me that if I had a chance at being normal, I wouldn't want to stick out again in my small, white-bread Lutheran town in country Australia with – gasp – dark skin?!

My mum has dark skin. She's South African – classed as a coloured in apartheid terms. Her skin is like brown sugar, chocolate milk, iced coffee. She and my dad, a white-skinned Englishman, courted illegally for four years under the apartheid regime. Apartheid was the racial segregation of people in South Africa, a policy that began in 1948 and lasted until the early 1990s. Apartheid meant that black and coloured people were institutionally segregated from white people.

My parents moved to Australia in the early 1980s, to escape apartheid so they could get married. I was born soon after. Mum was the only permanent black resident in Walla Walla. There were a few black exchange students at the private high school, but, as far as I know, she was the only black person to settle in Walla Walla in the fourteen or so years that we lived there.

Mum's skin is ageless. A bit like my skin – though for different genetic reasons. The smell of Oil of Olay is long gone from Mum's dresser. She doesn't rely on beauty products to keep herself looking youthful.

A few years ago, while sitting in the emergency department – I had cut my thumb severely – I said to Mum that I thought her neck needed a bit of moisturiser. She pulled at her neck and said, 'No. I've always had great skin. It's never been a problem.'

'Thanks for passing it on to me,' I chided. We both began to laugh, which encouraged those patients who overheard our exchange to smile too.

My parents have black skin and white skin. My skin tone isn't midway; it's red. It's so far from the exotic complexion I could have had.

I don't feel black. I don't feel white. How does being those skin colours feel, anyway?

It took me a long time to identify as 'Carly with the red skin'. My colour was so often associated with rude nicknames such as 'traffic light' and 'Redheads match'. I just wanted to be 'normal'.

But how else would you describe my face? Red is a fair and factual descriptor. Not an insult. Not derogatory. Just a fact.

I asked others with ichthyosis how they see themselves, especially if they are red (there are many types of ichthyosis, and it presents in different ways – sometimes noticeable and sometimes not). A couple recognised their colour, said it was a fact, similar to me. Some didn't want to see their colour, and that was often to do with other people's reactions – they were called derogatory names, or told they ruined school photos, or accused of being sunburnt or dirty. Some were very defensive and wouldn't answer. Some who are red, like me, saw themselves as white, because that's their ethnicity.

I'm in touch with many ichthyosis families through social media. I got chatting to a parent about this topic. She asked her son, who was almost thirteen, how he saw himself. The family is white and lives in North Carolina. Her son found this question confronting. He was unsure how to answer, perhaps because he had never considered the question before. Eventually he described himself as reddish. His mother thought he'd see himself like everyone else, and believes that maybe he is aware of nuances beyond his skin colour and ethnicity.

My geneticist confirmed that there's a typical facial structure for people with ichthyosis. High-set foreheads. Outwardly turned eyes. Round faces. When I meet someone with ichthyosis – especially Netherton syndrome, the type I have – I feel like they're my sibling. They look like my relative. We can finish one another's sentences like family.

I've been thinking about my culture. I often feel like a fraud. I didn't grow up learning Afrikaans or listening to rap as my South African friends did. But I knew something of the culture. South African curries were a staple meal. I learnt about Steve Biko and Nelson Mandela, and I called my parents' close friends uncle and aunty, even though they weren't relatives. My dad's English accent rubbed off on me a little, and I knew a lot about the Liverpool Football Club, too. But I sort of just felt Australian. What I knew best was Aussie pop culture and barbeques and running through the sprinkler in the summer. My parents encouraged this identification. Just before I started school, they were insistent I get one of my Australian 'aunties' to teach me the national anthem so I could sing it at assembly.

Mum's experience with skin is different from mine. She hasn't considered her colour as part of her identity like I have, she tells me. But like me, she believes it's up to others to accept our differences. That is changing yourself to fit in.

I've been saying I've got black heritage more and more. I call out racism, but I worry I'm so red people won't think I have authority to speak on the subject. Not that it matters – I should call out racism no matter what colour I am, of course.

I worry that Rachel Dolezal has made it hard for people like me to talk about race. Rachel Dolezal is an ethnically white woman who claimed to be black for years before she was exposed. She wears her hair in dreadlocks and has artificially tanned her face. But her background is not black. She has made it hard to talk about race if you don't look like you're from the particular racial group you're speaking about. And is racism even my burden to take on, when I don't identify as either black or white? The online discussions around race, and when to speak up or stay silent, make me frightened to be part of the conversation. I fear I am a phony to claim blackness when I haven't lived my mother's black culture and I haven't experienced the racism she did under apartheid.

Yet in recent years, I've been called a woman of colour by other people – sometimes because of my redness, and sometimes by some people who know my black heritage. If they see me that way, I give myself permission to see myself that way, too. I'm talking to and reading more from black women, and the more I read and hear about their experiences, the more I want to learn. I relate to some of their experiences because of mine, with disability and discrimination, but I also know that this might be a false equivalence and I don't want to presume to know what the daily experience of being a black woman is really like. Whiteness and blackness are more than skin colour – they're about levels of privilege. I find it hard to talk about race as a factor in the ableism and discrimination I face. I recognise my privilege in living in a country that is somewhat progressive when it comes to disability. In some cultures, disability and facial differences are seen as a curse, something to be ashamed about and hidden away. I don't want to tear down another marginalised group while talking about my own oppression. But if there's a place at the table for me, I'll listen.

Culturally, I feel like a middle-class white woman. I live in inner Melbourne. I listen to Aussie rock music. I earn a decent wage. I'm married and have travelled internationally. But I have felt discriminated against because of my skin colour – perhaps in similar and in different ways to my black family and friends. And I also see my skin as my identity, finally.

I look at my family: we're a melting pot of South African and English, and my husband is Malaysian-Australian. And those ichthyosis genes have created a uniqueness and bond that only a few others in the world understand.

After years of wanting to be different – or different from my difference – I have come to love my colour. My colour as a fashion accessory. As a talking point. As a culture. And after so many told me that I should be ashamed of my colour, I embrace it.

Trauma Is a Time Traveller

Ahmed Yussuf

I

In April 2018, before accusations of sexual harassment make him a controversial figure, Dominican-American writer Junot Díaz publishes an essay that contains a heartfelt revelation of childhood trauma.

He uses the phrase *trauma is a time traveller*.

It evokes something in you.

It is perhaps your story. The story of your father. The story of your family.

It is the moment that still follows you: the first failure of many in your black, overweight husk of a body.

The words stay for days – in your mind, in your spirit. So much so that you write them down several times.

Trauma is a time traveller, trauma is a time traveller, trauma is a time traveller.

2

You struggled after birth. Your father told you this, once.

You wonder if the world was hinting at the struggles to come. Your body lacked nourishment, was sickly and thin.

Your body is no longer thin, but still has all the ailments the newborn had.

Trauma is a time traveller.

3

You tell yourself, *Your body is not your own, you do not belong to it.*

You walk, talk and exist in a permanent failed state.

Trauma is a time traveller.

And that memory – this body and its failure – is crystallised as your father carries you, calling out for your mother.

She was fleeing a home resembling the pain and trauma your father once tried to escape.

He didn't know it would follow him wherever he was to go.

You ask yourself why you were not able to rustle away from his grip, away from his hands. Hands that have the violent residue of war all over them.

In this moment, you feel weightless in your father's arms. You watch your sister turn and leave, quickly, through the back door, to get to your mother. Her body, and her wit to find a way out, while you get stuck in between where you are and where you so desperately want to be.

Your body is still in the moment. It needs to be free.

4

You are taught how to be a good Muslim boy.

Your first lesson is *don't ask, just do*. You diligently follow.

You are fasting your first full month of Ramadan. You are staying with your mother's sister in Nairobi. You have completed the day, and now you are stuffing your face with all the food you have deprived yourself of.

You hear a knock on the door.

You see your aunt open it, and greet this man; he is her friend. He walks into the small apartment, and the two of you exchange handshakes and smiles.

You are invited to go to the *masjid*, the mosque, to pray Tarawih. You eagerly stroll through the sometimes muddy streets of Nairobi.

You are at the *masjid*. It is time to perform the Isha prayer. Your stomach feels strange, but you ignore the sounds. You make your wuḍū, cleaning your hands, arms, mouth, nostrils, feet. You begin the prayer.

Between rakats, units of prayer, you feel a surge of waste shoot out of your mouth.

You have desecrated the place of worship.

You are afraid. You wonder: what will happen? You think back to your first lesson: don't ask, just do. You *do*. You continue praying, on the floors of the *masjid* that have your evening meal all over them.

You feel pious. You are performing prayer under the harshest of conditions. You are following in the footsteps of the Prophet Muhammad and his companions.

Your second lesson is *silence*.

You have not learnt it yet, so they teach it to you.

You are at home. Your *mualim*, teacher, has come to teach you Qur'an. You have not practised your readings; you have not memorised your surah.

You are called to recite. You begin. You stumble. He hits you with the twig he picked up as he entered your home. Your fingers are red.

He asks you to continue. You stumble. He hits you again, this time on your arm. He asks you to continue. You stumble.

He hits you again, on your arm and hand.

You are holding back the tears. You cannot say anything: to speak back means more violence. You do not want more violence.

Your body is a painting of colours. You learn that your place is in silence.

5

At the age of fourteen, your body fails in a way that will define your life. *Trauma is a time traveller*. You are diagnosed with type 1 diabetes: a disease you qualify whenever someone asks about it.

It's not the type that happens when you are overweight.

Sure.

You watch them look at you and your body with a patronising stare.

In the classroom, pain and suffering are the lessons of the day. It is a space where black bodies are disposable. To be taunted less aggressively is a mercy you must always be grateful for: a mercy you try to convince yourself is a sign of friendship.

You search for survival. You adopt a mask to hide the bruises across your face. The scars are carved from the sharpness of adolescent bullying. You are hidden behind the shame of being you.

Trauma is a time traveller.

You tell yourself this mask was made to shield your body. The only medication at your disposal is bravado: masculinity. It is the best treatment available.

You hear more words in a passing interview: *blackness was never supposed to survive*.

Your survival will be all the things you're not.

Your high-school teacher speaks about your endowment falling out of your shorts, says you are exactly what people say about black men.

But you are still a black boy.

You become hollow, like an empty gift wrapper.

Trauma is a time traveller.

6

You are afraid to unmask the meaning of this body. You cannot recall a time where you and the mask weren't one. You teach yourself that you cannot have spring without reckoning winter's pain.

Back in the classroom, you are given a new name.

You are 'Abdi' because all the black people are the Abdis. You understand why they call you this: 'Abdi' means 'slave' in Arabic.

All the black people are slaves, in their minds.

Blackness was never meant to survive.

Trauma is a time traveller.

You fail again.

You are not musical, or sporting.

You do not possess this strange cocktail of coolness that *they*, the arbiters of blackness, wish you had.

You are an unruly fat body, diseased with diabetes.

You learn through these lessons that they are more black than you. Whatever 'black' is supposed to be.

You are edited out of your own story.

7

You have just finished a meal. You feel the weight of the plate's contents sliding through your stomach as it begins digesting. Your frame grows larger. You rush to the bathroom. You are on your knees, facing down, as your meal finds a new place out of your body.

This becomes your holy practice.

Trauma is a time traveller.

You like how your stomach feels as it empties. Emptiness is a feeling you crave.

Your body was never made to be a sacred place. *Blackness was never meant to survive*. It is a cage: a prison full of the deepest of emotions. You begin the cleansing process to force the food out of your insides. You need to strip away the glut from your body. Free yourself of the excess, free yourself of yourself.

You understand that to be African, to be black, is to mould your body unrelentingly.

Your uninhabitable body holds you back as the world beckons. It is a firmly fixed anchor: a boulder placed on your frail back, causing a stagger as you step.

You are not to be what you need to be.

8

You are unequipped to handle this mandate, in a body more akin to a prison. You attempt to strip away the ugliness you exist in. To strip away the stretches marked on your skin.

Your remedy is overmedication. Your insulin needle becomes your way out.

You test your body – how much it can take before it collapses. You wonder why it won't just stop. Why you cannot exit. You sit on the couch in your living room. There's nobody around, just you and the needle, and all the pain you want to go away.

You try to learn how to survive.

You slim down. Your body is not unruly anymore. You look in the mirror, where the marks once were.

You cannot unsee them.

Trauma is a time traveller.

9

You think back to that first failure: the moment in between the exit and your father's arms.

Vietnamese-American poet Ocean Vuong writes: *your father is only your father until one of you forgets.*

Trauma is a time traveller.

Blackness was never meant to survive.

Your father is only your father until one of you forgets.

You and your father have understood each other only through idle chit-chat and through conflict.

You rush outside barefoot, with your sisters and your mother. It is dark and cold. You are on the lookout for a phone box to find sanctuary. Your mother finds one. She calls her friend, asking if you all can stay at her house.

You want to be back: before the violence, before his anger, before those holes in the wall and that growing ache in your heart.

Forgetting becomes a source of great hope for you. You wonder if your body is only your body until you forget.

Trauma is a time traveller.

Forgetting is the way you understand your world. You practise it religiously.

One day, you are in a room with friends. They ask you about your childhood, and you think back to the moment with your father, and other moments where the fear of violence against your body, and the destruction of other bodies, those you care for deeply, was evoked.

You are no longer a child. You are taller and bigger than your father. You begin to assert yourself, to turn the violence away with more violence. You won't admit it to yourself, but you have stopped loving the man who held you as an infant. *Trauma is a time traveller.*

You push him. You are about to fight when your mother stops you. You remember the days when your world was splintering: all the intervention orders, all the police calls, the pain in your mother's eyes.

You cry uncontrollably.

Trauma is a time traveller.

10

Your body betrays you once again.

You see no tissues: all you have is a sleeve, and a room awash with sympathy.

You speak. You feel heard. You are open about who you are and what you want to be.

11

You now try to practise kindness, to yourself, to others. You try to understand the *this*; you try to understand how trauma travels through time. You try to understand that your story is your story. You try to understand that you may never love your body completely, but your mission is to come as close as possible.

You are past the high-school bullies, the toxic friendships, the people in your life who try to define your body. But you still struggle. Finished meals make you uncomfortable. You long for your former religious practice. You understand this process isn't easy, that you will not be magically cured of your pain. Trauma still haunts you like a ghost in the night.

Trauma is a time traveller.

Dear Australia, I Love You But …

Candy Bowers

Dear Australia,
I love you but …
You've been a really shit foster parent.
I thought I'd just lay that out flat, like that, like
   I practised in therapy.
You. Are. Not. My. Real. Dad.
But we are family, so here's what I need you to know:
This sister with her fat booty found it difficult to grow
   up in a country where beauty was exclusively based on
   blonde hair and white skin,
Where long skinny legs were the thing,
And flat, board-like bums awkwardly swung.
The invisibility stung.
In high school, *Home and Away* beach babes haunted
   my dreams.
That's what you let me watch on TV?
And then at fifteen you bought me that subscription to
   Dolly magazine.
I desperately wanted to look like an Aussie cover girl,
   Caucasian, freckled, stick-skinny and sweet like
   strawberry cream.
But every teenage part of me was the opposite of that.

I was brown, coconut-round, afro, hands-on-curvaceous-
    hips fat.
My adolescent subconscious did the maths,
Australia,
Dad,
You set me up.

What I'm talking about here is a consistent attack on
    my body image and self-esteem.
How's a little afro-black girl meant to identify or
    visualise when she can't see herself reflected:
Booty,
Hips,
Or goddamn thick-thighs?
How can she feel comfortable when she doesn't fit into
    jeans at Sportsgirl or Surf, Dive 'n Ski?
Like her mama and her mama's mama and a large part
    of her community,
This afro-black girl had a naturally fat body,
Since day one of primary school,
Since 1983.
Your message was consistent,
White and thin equals beautiful,
Black and fat equals unimportant and ugly,
Or simply put
It was unacceptable to look like me.
The constant othering damaged my soul.
Australia, you stole years as I tried to be smaller and
    whiter and less bold.

So fuck you, Dad,

Why would I be interested in hugging it out or waiting
for you to get it?

I grew up feeling like my body was wrong and the pants
were right.

No matter how hurt,

I had to fight,

For my womanhood and my worth,

Which tips into a whole other letter about your bullshit
misogyny

Because from parliament to hip-hop to film to media to
boardrooms

Australia is nowhere near gender equality,

As white men dominate and colonise daily in your toxic
image.

But right now,

Let's stick to this particular bullshit, shall we.

You like to call yourself the lucky country,

And yet I had to excavate and travel through mazes and
break through walls to find guides to keep me from
drowning in the sea of toxicity you built around me.

The authors I was looking for didn't exist in Australian
bookshops or libraries.

Growing up African in Australia before black Google, black
Twitter and black Instagram was oppressively cruel.

Music pointed the way,

Referencing the higher black female thought I needed to
fill my plate.

Lucky for Adeva, Monie Love, Queen Latifah,
   Salt-N-Pepa
And TLC.
Lucky for Alice Walker, Audre Lorde, Lebo Mashile,
   Angela Davis, Maya Angelou
And Suzan-Lori.
Lucky for Tiddas, Oodgeroo, Christine Anu
And KillaQueenz.
And lucky for Candy B.
Lucky for me,
Hijacking the stage and fucking with your system,
Rewiring,
Reclaiming,
Rewriting herstory.

Re-parenting myself was tough,
Like any sort of domestic violence, the rebuild is plagued
   with self-doubt, pain and confusion.
But I did it.

So Dad,
You racist oppressive dangerous colonising misogynist
   soul-destroying piece of shit,
As I detach from this embedded attachment in which my
   identity is tangled with yours and I feel like a visitor
   in my own family and I can't stand people who
   celebrate the day you invaded and stole this land and
   I feel sorry for those trying to reconcile with you
   because you might have said sorry but what's sorry
   without accountability, or action, or treaty, and I can't
   feel comfortable anywhere and I don't even know why

I'm telling you all this because you're not listening and
   you don't care.

Like anything one ever writes to a perpetrator,
It's more for themselves than the reader;
Like fancy food eaten quickly by hungry children was to
   the cook or the feeder.

I am no longer your child or student.
My teachers are black women,
Poets, musicians, writers, artists, activists and
   philosophers from across the world,
First people,
And me.

To all those little afro-black girls still growing up
   invisible,
Still seeking reflection,
I see you.
My triumphs will change you
More than my hurt,
I didn't write this for him,
Little sisters feel it,
For you are my words.

CHANGEMAKERS

Profiled

Daniel Haile-Michael

It was November 2005. We were playing basketball at our local court at the housing estate in Flemington. Most people were out and about. They had broken their Ramadan fast. We were just spending time around the neighbourhood, playing ball. I was with three people, and one of the guys wanted to grab a cigarette. We walked from the housing estates out onto the main street, where the petrol station was. The petrol station was about 100 metres from the local high school. It just happened to be muck-up day.

After we got the cigarettes, we continued walking up the main road, almost past the high school. We saw what looked like security guards at the entrance to the school, so we thought, *Let's go back, let's go back onto the estates.*

We started going back down to the estates, but by the time we got to the petrol station, a divvy van pulled up and swerved in front of us. Two cops got out. They said, 'What are you bloody idiots doing in the school?'

They alleged that we had been inside the grounds throwing rocks, or something like that. We told them we had nothing to do with whatever they were talking about. They didn't believe us.

It escalated quickly. It just started really going off. They began to physically assault us, punching and kicking.

I was scared for my life. It was hard to comprehend what was happening at the time. I never thought someone who was supposed to protect you would assault and batter you. I was fifteen, not doing anything wrong, and being assaulted by police officers.

My biggest fear was what they were going to do next. I thought, *If they are doing this in public, once they arrest me, what's going to happen then? If I don't get away from these cops right now, I'm in trouble.* That was the scariest thing. That was what was running through my mind.

When the officers hit me, I yelled and screamed, to see if people could come and help, come and assist us. No one was around.

After the assault, it got real for me. A lot of my friends had been complaining about police harassment, but I sort of just thought they were in the wrong place or they were doing the wrong thing, and it was no big deal. Or maybe they were just exaggerating, like young guys do. Then it happened to me, and it was very real. I became a lot more fearful of police, and of law enforcement in general. I felt uncomfortable.

I stopped walking places. When I did walk somewhere, I tried to avoid going alone; I went with friends. I tried to avoid situations where I might be alone with law enforcement. I can't remember where I was living at the time, but I think I started taking a different route to school as well. I avoided main roads; 'always take the back way' became my motto.

I didn't tell my family. They wouldn't have believed me. They might have suspected that I actually did something wrong; they always took the side of the system. They are very grateful for having moved to Australia. Given their refugee background, they think everything is perfect here. It's very hard for them to imagine that something like this could happen. Australia is supposed to be an ideal country. Sometimes they say, 'Just toughen up.' Like this is nothing, compared to what might go on in other places.

We used to go to this youth drop-in centre in North Melbourne. I was known as the good boy, the nerd of the whole neighbourhood. And when that happened to me, everyone at the centre started talking about it. They told the youth workers. Then, on one of the drop-in nights, the workers stopped all the activities and said we needed to create a youth leadership group to try to deal with some of these issues that were happening in the neighbourhood. People put their hands up to join.

From that night, we teamed up with the council on a voluntary basis to try to come up with a few initiatives that could solve some of the issues affecting our community: unemployment, discrimination, poverty.

We developed a relationship with the local legal centre to work on the issue of law enforcement. The five of us who had been harassed by police officers launched a court case against Victoria Police. It was to do with racial profiling.

The case lasted from 2005 to 2013. Eight years. The way the justice system is set up, these processes are so arduous and long. We didn't go to court straight off; there was a lot of negotiation, a lot of going through different bodies, first.

Sometimes it was frustrating to deal with this because I just wanted to move on and try to live a normal life. But in many ways I couldn't, because there was always this unresolved thing there; I always reflected on that one time I was so vulnerable and so scared. There was trauma. I was in a constant, almost continuous, state of fear. In some ways, I was on a military mission: every day you just want to get through it, survive.

Other times I'd have to sacrifice my time, and my money, and my energy just trying to deal with the case and the issue of racial profiling more broadly. Attending community meetings, and doing all that kind of activism stuff at such a young age – it was tough. I constantly felt conflicted between doing what was important and what was right for me, and doing what was right for the community. It felt like I had put my life on pause to follow this thing that needed to be done.

People pulled out during those eight years. Some felt it was too taxing. They didn't see a benefit for them and their communities in the short term. When the burden became too much, they gave up. For Victoria Police, the case was important because it was about improving their systems and their processes. For the lawyers, well, that is their careers. But for us, as the individuals in the case, we were being asked to put our lives on hold for no individual gain. For some, that was a high price to pay, especially given the situation we were in – it's not as if we were middle class, you know, and had a house, had these basic things you need to survive as a human. We were vulnerable. We had grown up in a housing commission: first-generation refugees who were trying to establish a life in a new home. It was a big thing that was being asked of us in that context.

For me, the personal toll entailed not having the space and time and energy to excel in my studies, and to get myself out of poverty quickly. Those years I spent volunteering and helping the community out and being expected to take on leadership roles, all the advocacy work – that was unpaid for many years, at a time when I was supposed to be establishing my life and trying to do things like purchase a home, get a stable job, start a career. I don't regret it, but I sort of turned between those two worlds. I was doing a civil engineering degree, and all this community work on the side. It's hard to really excel in anything in that situation; I compromised on both.

In 2013, the police settled the case with us. In some ways I felt relief at the settlement, but there was also a bit of regret.

Because I really wanted to see the police officers get on the stand to explain why they did what they did. The officers had actually retired, so that was not going to happen, I knew that. But I felt like it should've happened; I wanted to see them in court, having to explain their actions to a judge. On the other hand, we had people drop out from our case, and it had been so many years since those incidents, so if we were called to the stand our memories wouldn't have been as clear as they could have been. There were are all these other factors that blurred our chances of success were we to go to trial.

I think, in the end, what the case did for Victoria, and what it's done for Australia, is really progress the discussion on issues of police discrimination and racial profiling. If you look at it on a systemic level, the case became a pivotal point – it sort of pushed the state to really try to address some of these issues. To that end, I think, it was a good result.

In 2015, two years after the settlement, my co-defendant Maki Issa and I released a report: 'The More Things Change, the More They Stay the Same'. It looks at police treatment of ten men of African and refugee backgrounds in Flemington, Sunshine, Noble Park and Dandenong. The report made clear that while Victoria Police had made changes to address racial profiling, new patterns of behaviour were not occurring across the organisation. The *Herald Sun* reported, correctly, that we were 'shocked by the extent that police inflicted serious assault, harassment and public ridicule on young African men, as well as by how widely accepted the practices were within their communities'.

Releasing that report felt good. I mean, in the sense that I sort of felt vindicated. At least I did something for society. When you risk so much to change something, when you see some progress, you sort of feel like, *Yeah, this is worth it.* That in itself was a huge reward.

In terms of racial profiling of African-Australians now, in some ways we are back where we were ten years ago or more. But I think a lot of things have changed, too. Ten years ago I might not have had politicians standing up against the kind of police profiling that happened to me, whereas now at least there is a certain section of society who have a better understanding of what racial profiling is, and who aren't afraid to call it out. I feel like within the leadership of Victoria Police ten years ago, they would have just supported one another. In February 2018, the assistant commissioner was found to have sent racist messages outside of work time, using a pseudonym, and he resigned. I don't think that would have happened ten years ago. It would have just been in the media for a little bit, with no other consequences. Whereas now you've got the leadership team who's – if we're looking at it from the outside – actually saying that these sorts of things aren't on, that you can't make those racist comments. I think there's less room now for intolerance than there was ten years ago.

Given where I am today, what happened to me sometimes doesn't seem like such a big deal anymore. But you know, if I wasn't as resilient as I was, and if I didn't have the right support people around me, and if I couldn't move out of that neighbourhood, if I was locked there, I could have easily seen myself going down a road where I'd constantly be in contact with the justice system. I'd have a life that was trapped in cycles of fear, and be in and out of jail. Thank goodness I got out of that place. The fact that I am where I am, I feel okay. But if things hadn't lined up for me, I think that would have completely destroyed my life.

For a lot of my peers, that's been the case. A lot of them are just in and out of jail now. That sort of police profiling really criminalised a lot of my friends. It's very hard. You wish you had the resources to assist, to get them out of that environment. To get them away from the situation, because you know what it's like, but you're kind of helpless.

I'm twenty-eight now, and the case is six years behind me. I feel like I've progressed beyond it. I feel like I've done my bit, and have seen other young people who have been inspired by that work and made advocacy a career for themselves. In the local African community we have social workers, we have lawyers; it sort of feels like there are enough people now, and there's a real movement that's being built against police harassment. It feels like there is hope.

The Dangers of a Single Story

Tariro Mavondo

It is a Saturday morning on Ramsay Street. The sound of a lawnmower is drowned out by the diesel hum of a removalist truck blasting a Bollywood tune as it turns into Australia's most famous cul-de-sac. Don't like the look of the new Indian neighbours? Too bad: it's 2012, and the Kapoors, the conspicuous new residents of the much-loved soap opera *Neighbours*, are here to stay.

Ramsay Street's newest family is part of a deliberate campaign to diversify Australia's favourite neighbourhood. The move has already met with public outrage: online comments criticising Channel 10's decision have been filled with racist vitriol. Me? Well, I just hope that the Kapoor children have better luck in suburban Australia than I did.

The only black kid in my neighbourhood, I was forced to undergo a gruelling initiation into life in contemporary suburbia. Once, I was desperate to play hide-and-seek with the other neighbourhood kids, but Matthew Scubble, the self-appointed lead in a cast of bullies, had other ideas: I was forced to drink his urine before I was allowed to participate.

Another popular game was to yank at my beaded extension braids as I walked past. The aim was to successfully uproot the hair extensions, and my scalped braids became collector's items. Scubble and his gang were oblivious to the tears streaming down my face.

When I was around ten, *The Fresh Prince of Bel-Air* began screening. I was so grateful to see a young black face on television. Trying to emulate actor Will Smith's coolness – and desperate to climb the social ladder – I attempted a schoolyard rap:

> *Yo! My name is Tariro, I think I'm so cool*
> *All the children in the block want to hear my new rule*
> *If you want to play it funky, then you better play with me*
> *I'm the best in the world and you're gonna get it free.*

Needless to say, I failed miserably.

I also remember, with great clarity, my first experience seeing a black woman on an Australian television series. With her shoulder-length frizzy curls and long slender legs, Stephanie Mboto strolled along the sandy beach of *Home and Away*'s Summer Bay in 1996. My twelve-year-old self was startled and delighted at our resemblance. Stephanie was like me. A young refugee from Somalia, she had smuggled her way into Summer Bay in the hope of being looked after by a resident who had earlier served as a peacekeeper in her war-torn homeland. Local teenagers Liam Tanner and Casey Mitchell quickly took her under their wing, and Stephanie and Liam became a couple.

My adolescent self was totally hooked, and it came as a complete surprise when Stephanie met her untimely end. Having gone adventuring with some of the other teenagers, *Home and Away*'s first African character ended up dangling from the edge of a cliff and eventually falling to her death.

Life is like that in Summer Bay – the buff, blond men surf the big waves, the skinny, bronzed chicks stroll the beach in string bikinis and the black refugees plummet to their deaths.

Unlike *Neighbours'* Australianised Kapoor family, Stephanie Mboto had entered Australia illegally: a queue jumper on a fake passport. And in an Australian soap, certain doom has a way of finding such impostors.

It's now fourteen years since that cliffside death, and I'm about to become one of the first African-born acting graduates of the Victorian College of the Arts. While channel surfing, I stumble across another Stephanie Mboto in Summer Bay. This time her name is Grace Johnson and she is involved in residency fraud, marrying Polynesian-Australian Elijah Johnson to secure proper medical treatment for her very ill son. Instead of falling off a cliff, Grace is punished by her son's premature death. The government then uncovers Grace's deception; in her final appearance on screen, she desperately pleads to stay in Australia while being carted off by immigration officials.

Watching, I find myself wondering if these are the only roles I will play, if the desperate 'illegal other' is the only way Australian viewers will accept racial and cultural diversity on television. If so, then were all my wonderful blind-casted roles at drama school pointless? Is there any value in playing Blair from Michael Gurr's *Perfume, Underwear and Crash Helmet*, Nina from Chekhov's *The Seagull* and Desdemona from Shakespeare's *Othello*? What use is my vocal and technical training if I'm destined only to play a doomed refugee with a generic 'African' accent?

I start wondering if I should think seriously about moving abroad in search of stage and screen opportunities.

It is a perfect sunny day. The waiters at the riverside café are smiling and chatting. It is lunchtime and the place is filling up with men and women in business suits and corporate apparel. I'm with Wahibe Moussa, a bubbly and attractive Lebanese-Australian actor and writer. Wahibe and I met a few months earlier, at a Melbourne International Arts Festival and Multicultural Arts Victoria masterclass exploring refugee-based documentary theatre. We choose a seat in the shade and order some grilled eggplant to share. She is bursting with enthusiasm, only too happy to discuss issues of visibility, representation and cultural diversity on Australian television.

'There is a myth underpinning the fabric of our nation,' Wahibe says. 'A myth that Australia is a clean country, a tidy place, because we haven't had a civil war. This myth permeates all aspects of Australian life, including our entertainment industry.'

This idea takes me aback, but I lean in closer, absorbed by what she is saying.

'When migrants come to this country we enter into an invisible contract, an understanding to keep Australia clean. An artist's role is to remind other Australians of the mud under this veneer of civilisation, because the reality is that it is cracking.'

Wahibe is so impassioned by what she is saying that she knocks over the salt-and-pepper shakers, making me laugh. But we soon get serious again.

'Look at the political structures set up in this society and what it is doing to people. Look at the inhumane treatment of refugees. Look at the fact that whenever public debates about Indigenous Australians get real, people go blind again and bury their heads.'

A truck pulls up nearby and drowns out our conversation. Wahibe apologises for the noise and then continues. 'As artists we cannot – indeed, we *must* not – take it for granted that Australians are unaware of their own political climate, because we run the risk of hitting people over the head with material. This is harmful to our growth as a nation.'

As she says this, I can't help but picture scenes from well-intentioned fringe theatre works I've both attended and participated in. Several months ago, I and two other African-Australian women stood at the top of the steep stairs dividing the auditorium at Federation Square's BMW Edge (now Deakin Edge). Descending towards the stage slowly and mournfully, we sang the old Negro spiritual 'Sometimes I Feel like a Motherless Child'. The three of us are members of Stillwaters, a storytelling group for women of African descent, and we were performing a short musical choreo-poem as part of a multicultural dialogue at the annual The Light in Winter festival. One young black woman in each aisle, we moved slowly towards a seated panel, each person representing a different part of the world, but collectively symbolising the Australian multicultural story. When we reached the stage and turned to face the audience, I was disappointed to see no more than thirty people sparsely populating the 200 or so seats.

'Our role is to show the citizens of our nation ways of going beyond the parameters we have collectively set ourselves. We need to let ourselves be burnt in order to grow from our infancy as a nation.' Wahibe's voice cuts through my thoughts. The glaring stage lights of BMW Edge flicker, and I am brought back to our discussion in the café.

The phrase 'we need to let ourselves be burnt in order to grow' keeps ringing in my ears as I return home from the interview. I plonk myself tiredly on the lounge and absentmindedly switch on the television. The SBS tagline, 'six billion stories and counting', glows.

On screen, vibrant psychedelic patterns morph in and around one another. African children are singing in a familiar vernacular over African drumming. A received-pronunciation English voice rides over the other sounds, informing viewers about Toumtaka, a village in Africa.

'Six billion stories and counting.'

I think about how the experiences of Stephanie Mboto and Grace Johnson don't reflect my own story. I think about how none of the billions of stories told on SBS seem to mirror the story of African skilled migrants. My father was the head of Zimbabwe Polytech, one of the country's largest and oldest colleges. After the White Australia Policy, as part of a drive to recruit skilled migrants from across the Commonwealth, my father was offered an academic position in Monash University's School of Business and Marketing. He accepted the post, and two years later the rest of my family – my mother, my older brother, my two younger sisters and I – followed his journey to the land down under.

The destination: Frankston.

It was a difficult move. We had belonged to the higher echelon of Zimbabwean society and we lost our life of affluence: gardeners, cooks, housekeepers and nannies. We arrived in the neighbourhood streets of Frankston with next to nothing. I remember faintly the day we woke up early and left our big house in Marondera, a city about 72 kilometres east of Harare. Even at the age of five, I remember feeling with absolute certainty that something very big was happening.

Something very big did happen: I grew up with dual identities. Visually I am African, but culturally I am a hybrid: Vegemite is my favourite spread, Ugg boots and flannelette shirts among my most worn apparel. I have an Aussie accent, yet I dance like my spirit has never left my motherland, and I was gifted with a deep, resonant singing voice.

'Six billion stories and counting.'

I want to see African-Australians like me in Australian television shows: a female surfing champion in Summer Bay, or a teenager over the Ramsay Street fence – ordinary neighbours who just happen to be black. I want to see me. And I can't see what's so controversial about that.

Out of the relative whitewashing of the Australian story there occasionally leaps some colour. SBS's *Kick* is set in the Melbourne suburb of Brunswick and follows the lives of a multicultural neighbourhood that includes Lebanese-Australian, Greek-Australian, Anglo-Australian, Serbian-Australian and Vietnamese-Australian families. The ABC's highly acclaimed eight-part miniseries *The Slap*, an adaptation of Christos Tsiolkas's novel of the same name, is small-screen diversity at its best, showing Greek-Australians, Asian-Australians and Australians of colour co-existing in the inner-city suburbs as a matter of fact, rather than a political statement. A huge part of this series's success is the fact that the writer is Greek-Australian.

But even initiatives such as Blacktown City Council's African Theatre Project and Melbourne's Stillwaters storytelling group – projects dedicated to increasing the diversity of voice and representation in Australian writing, stage and television – cannot work alone to get their stories heard by a mass audience.

In Australia, some lobby and industry groups are making headway on diversity and representation. In 2012, Actors Equity secured agreement from the Screen Producers Association of Australia (SPAA) and Live Performance Australia (LPA) to attach a 'colourblind casting policy' to their contracts with directors and casting consultants. Actors Equity was in discussions with SPAA about maintaining records and collecting statistics relating to ethnicity, gender and disability for all auditions, interviews and hirings. SPAA and LPA were also supportive of developing colourblind casting workshops to promote racially inclusive policies and behaviour.

A few months later, I'm thinking about blind casting, the discussion with Wahibe and the public backlash against *Neighbours'* new Indian-Australian residents as I'm selecting material to perform for Agent's Day, a mammoth end-of-year event where casting directors, casting agents, agents and directors are invited to a graduate showcase.

The right selection of material is almost as important as the performance itself. I wonder, with anguish, about whether to perform a culturally specific monologue – the West Indian spirit medium, for instance, or the African air spirit. I know this is probably my best bet for finding work quickly. I also fear that, if I take this route, I will one day become the cliff-dangling Stephanie Mboto or the deported Grace Johnson.

'Six billion stories and counting.' But where is mine?

....

It's mid-December 2011 and I am at the Melbourne Theatre Company's Lawler Studio. Butterflies beat in my stomach as I stand on the side of the stage, looking nervously out at the rows of seats filled by industry personnel. I'm standing with twenty-one other hopeful graduates, dressed in smart stage blacks. Piano keys start their opening tune, and the VCA's class of 2011 enters in small groups, singing and grooving to 'Mama Told Me Not to Come'.

In slow motion, I pick up a clear umbrella and a small black book. James, my scene partner, meets me in the centre of the stage. James transforms into Bill, a man getting drenched by the rain. Bill sees Betty, my character, under an umbrella. He begins to ask if he can share the umbrella with her, but she rejects him abruptly. Bill tries again, using the same words but a different approach. Again, he is knocked back. On the third attempt Bill is successful, and the pair move on to talk about the novel Betty is reading. Eventually they leave together to go on a date.

The scene is our adaptation of American playwright David Ives's *Sure Thing*. I am just a woman, under an umbrella, trying to read a Faulkner novel. It is incidental that I am black.

During the showcase, agents scribble notes about who they might be interested in putting on their books. At the following lunch banquet, and during the few agent interviews I attend, I'm spoken to candidly about how, though colourblind casting has been talked about for a while, it will be some time before it becomes the dominant model used in the Australian entertainment industry. It's refreshing to hear from one agency that they specifically put forward actors that directors wouldn't normally have in mind to challenge the status quo and to ensure those from culturally diverse backgrounds have the same opportunities as Anglo actors.

A few weeks later, exhausted from the stress that comes after Agent's Day, I turn on my computer and discover an email from Bell Shakespeare inviting me to audition for the lead female role in Molière's *The School for Wives*. The play is being directed by Lee Lewis as part of the company's 2012 program. I'm ecstatic, washed over with bliss. I am an Australian actor, about to audition for a lead role with one of Australia's premier ensembles. And I just happen to be African-Australian. I immediately read through the suggested audition scene and check the library's webpage to see if the book is available.

I later find out that three other VCA actors have been offered an audition for the role. There are stark differences in appearance between the four of us, and I hope in my heart of hearts that this is indeed indicative of blind casting at its best.

Weeks later, the audition is held in a rehearsal room at the Melbourne Theatre Company. I note again, with both hope and surprise, that the actor auditioning immediately before me has dark hair and an olive complexion.

The actor comes out of her audition, gives me a genuine smile and wishes me the best of luck. I begin repeating quietly to myself my personal mantra: 'How strong is your vision? Do you fear? Dare to take the risk!'

Lewis's friendly and professional assistant comes out, introduces herself and directs me to the audition room. I am greeted by Lewis's very casual and laidback manner as she invites me to take a seat to have a chat. Immediately she puts me at ease. We talk briefly about me and then the rest of the conversation is about the play.

The time comes to perform and Lewis asks me if I require a chair during the scene. I decline politely and begin the scene standing.

The audition goes well, but only time will tell whether Bell Shakespeare is ready to put a blind-cast African-Australian in a production.

I start my journey into the Australian acting industry open-eyed and wary, but also enthusiastic and hopeful.

....

It is a Saturday morning on Ramsay Street. The sound of gates shutting in white-picket fences combines with the chaotic jingle of front doors being locked frantically. African children sing in a familiar vernacular over African drumming. Two young black girls sit on a front porch, taking turns to thread beads onto each other's braids as they wait for the removalist van to arrive with their family's belongings. Don't like the look of the new African neighbours? Too bad: it's 2019, and the Deng family, the conspicuous new residents of Ramsay Street, are here to stay.

Not the Only One

Kamara Gray

My mother's memories of me dancing start in Port Moresby, a toddler grooving along to traditional Papua New Guinean dance.

My parents are of Jamaican heritage, and they grew up in London. In 1979, they moved to Papua New Guinea for work. This is where I was born, and spent my first three years. There was no television; in our household, my parents listened to the radio and their own music (rhythm and blues, soul, and reggae). We also went to watch live traditional dance and music performances. My mother says I was always ready to join in but was never 'over the top'. No diva tendencies back then!

After we moved to Sydney, I began to watch *Countdown*, a popular music-video show. My favourite music videos were 'Karma Chameleon' by Culture Club and 'Wake Me Up Before You Go-Go' by Wham! (It was the 1980s – don't judge me.) The Culture Club video had dancers, and some of them were black. I knew all the words and dance moves to those two songs, as well as to anything by Michael Jackson. I nagged my mum about going to dance classes, and was enrolled in weekly classes at age three. I started off with ballet and modern.

My first memory of being onstage was when I was around five years old. I was performing a tap-dance solo at the end-of-year concert for my dance school. I don't remember the song but I do remember the costume: a skirt, made from fringing. It was far too long, and my teacher wrapped it around and around my waist to make it fit, and then fastened it with a safety pin. As I began my solo, the skirt began to unravel in a train behind me. When the other dancers later joined me on stage, they had to play 'don't trip over Kamara's skirt', much to the delight of the audience. This didn't faze me at all because I enjoyed performing so much. I kept my head held high throughout the wardrobe malfunction and maintained a huge smile on my face as I carried on tapping, not missing a beat. I was onstage and my audience had expectations.

In primary school I enjoyed performing, whether dancing, acting or singing. I always knew everyone's parts and would sometimes whisper people's lines to them if they forgot the words – I thought I was being helpful, I suppose. I prided myself on always knowing the choreography to any dance number. My most notable performance, I think, was when I dressed up as Tina Turner and danced and lip-synced to 'Simply the Best'.

For many years, I attended a wonderful Sydney dance school called Bodenweiser Dance Centre, run by a woman named Margaret Chapple (known fondly as 'Chappie'). The school was an integral part of my development. I spent nearly every Saturday, and many an evening, there until my teenage years.

At the dance school I studied ballet, tap, modern and jazz. I was the only black student, but this was not something of which I was overly aware. It was 'normal' for me. Mostly, I felt supported and encouraged by the teachers. I was rarely made to feel that I was 'different', which reflected the attitudes of teachers and parents associated with the schools that I attended.

Yet ballet class was another story. Here I received more critique than the other students. My ballet teacher regularly told me to straighten my 'banana back' and to 'stick in my bottom'. Just where I should stick it, I didn't know. The teacher did not understand that my naturally curved body shape was due to my African heritage, and not something I could 'fix' or change. My mum was frustrated when such comments were made. Nevertheless, I continued with ballet, along with all the other dance styles.

As time went on, I began to particularly enjoy tap. Part of the appeal was that you didn't have to be a certain body shape or look to excel in the style. I'm not sure at what age I became aware of this, but it was definitely part of the appeal.

I had a fabulous African-American tap teacher named Ted Williams. He was hugely inspirational for me. He'd featured in the film *The Wiz* as one of the lead Munchkins. He was brilliant and exuberant, and I enjoyed tap even more thanks to his presence. When he returned to New York, I remained in contact with him.

When Chappie passed away, Bodenweiser unfortunately closed. I moved to a dance school near Bondi. Here, there were two other black dancers, sisters. For the first time, I was *not the only one*.

My family were members of a community organisation called the West Indian Association of Australia. Its members were individuals and families of West Indian heritage, or with a connection to West Indian culture. As a member of the group I was fortunate to learn folkloric songs and dances, which we would perform as a group at various cultural festivals and events. Through the organisation I was able to meet other Caribbean people of all ages. I was one of the younger dancers, and looked up to the older members. Being part of the group helped me to maintain a connection to my heritage, my culture and other people of Caribbean descent. Here, I was one of many.

I went to a selective high school, Sydney Girls' High. We had a supportive dance teacher, Ms Ghitgos, who encouraged us to perform and choreograph pieces. Each year our school entered the Rock Eisteddfod, a hotly contested national schools competition. Each school would create an eight-minute dance-based performance piece featuring up to 100 students. It was a prestigious competition, and our school would spend up to a year rehearsing and creating our piece. There were elaborate costumes, sets and choreography involved: it was serious business. I earnt several lead roles in our Rock Eisteddfod entries during the years I was at school.

My school was somewhat multicultural, but most of the non-Anglo students were of South-East Asian heritage. From a population of nearly 1000, there was only one other black student. She was a few grades above me, and when she graduated there was just me. As at dance school, I was aware of this fact, but it didn't overly faze me. Due to Rock Eisteddfod, I knew a lot of other students, across year groups. Dance was our common bond: the language in which we communicated and got to know one another. I joined in all the same activities as everyone else, including undergoing a stint on the rowing team (I only lasted one season). I even joined a cheerleading squad at one point! Of course, I was the only black dancer on the team. Upon reflection, I suspect they may have thought my presence unusual, but if they did, I wasn't aware.

I discovered the Alvin Ailey American Dance Theater and the Dance Theater of Harlem during my teenage years. These American ballet companies had either all or predominantly African-American dancers. I remember seeing in a local paper that one of the companies was coming to Melbourne to perform. I was determined to go and see them. I saved and saved to be able to attend, but I didn't end up saving enough for the fare from Sydney to Melbourne.

I found out that the Alvin Ailey American Dance Theater had a school in New York, and each year they ran a six-week summer school. I made it my mission to attend. Once I had completed my final year of high school, in 1997, I decided to defer university for one year. During that year, I applied for the Ailey school and got accepted to the summer program. I worked and saved so that I could go.

My first class at the Ailey school was life-changing. Never before had I seen black dancers doing ballet. I remember walking past an advanced ballet class and most of the students were black. They looked incredible. I was absolutely awestruck. In my first ballet class, my teacher looked like me. All of a sudden I could développé my leg, and lift it to the side, higher than I'd ever lifted it before. I had such an increased level of confidence in my own abilities after seeing that teacher. My other dance teachers had all made positive contributions to my development, but this was *different*. I had not appreciated the impact that being in an environment where there were teachers and other dancers of colour would have on me. It was far removed from the days of my 'banana back' ballet class. Everyone had different body shapes, and their skin covered a range of hues. That experience encouraged me to pursue dance professionally.

Following a year of travelling, I enrolled to study a Bachelor of Human Movement Studies. After quickly discovering that it was not the field for me (it was science-based, with no dance), I opted to instead study dance full-time. I was recommended a school in Melbourne called DanceWorld 301. After this, things moved very quickly. I travelled to Melbourne, auditioned, was accepted and arranged to move there a week later. I think my mum was surprised by the snap decision, but it was the right choice at the time.

While in Melbourne, I was offered the chance to dance in the opening ceremony of the Sydney Olympics. I ended up spending many a weekend travelling back to Sydney to rehearse. I performed as a lead tap dancer in the 'Eternity' section of the ceremony, which was choreographed by Dein Perry of *Tap Dogs* fame. Performing in the opening ceremony was unforgettable, and after that experience, I knew that I wanted to make a career from dancing.

Yet I had always enjoyed both academics and dancing, so after my year of full-time dance school, I went back to university – this time to study tourism management. I thought that if I didn't become a dancer, I could always work in a resort on a South Pacific island – not a bad alternative! I continued with dance classes and auditions alongside my studies, and I was offered a job dancing aboard a cruise ship, the P&O *Pacific Sky*. I transferred my degree to a university where I could study by correspondence, and accepted the job.

The role involved performing musical theatre–style productions in the onboard theatre. For nine months, as the ship travelled around New Zealand and the South Pacific, I not only danced professionally but also cruised around the beautiful region. A dream job. On my ship there was one other black staff member, a lady from Vanuatu. We regularly got mistaken for each other, even though I thought we looked nothing alike. (My own mother even mistook her for me one time. I never let my mum forget it!)

I was always keen to move to London, and following the end of the cruise-ship contract my mum suggested an extended six-month trip with the family. Well, six months turned into twelve months, which turned into years. Fifteen years later, we are still residing in London. When I first arrived, I enjoyed being around

Afro-Caribbean culture and people. Making a career from dance was challenging: there were certainly more opportunities in London, but there were also more dancers, and subsequently more dancers of colour. When I was auditioning in Sydney, on the dance circuit, there was one other black female dancer whom I knew of, and people would regularly ask me if I was her. Whereas in Australia I was once 'unique' and 'the only one' (or one of two), I was now one of many.

Nevertheless, I had some good career opportunities. I performed in film, television commercials and live events, including at the MTV Europe Music Awards, and in *L'heure espagnole* with the Royal Opera. I obtained most of these jobs through auditioning, which can be a challenging process at the best of times. You experience a lot of rejections along the way.

Alongside my dancing jobs I would teach to earn extra money. I eventually completed a teaching qualification with the British Ballet Organization, which led to a job teaching dance overseas at the British School of Kuwait for two years.

Back in London, I was watching a performance from a leading dance school with a relatively large student body. I noticed that there were less than a handful of brown faces onstage, which, considering the cultural diversity that exists within London, didn't seem right. In that moment, I was inspired to work out a way to provide opportunities to aspiring dancers of African and Caribbean descent, in a bid to somehow help to increase those numbers. Such dancers were underrepresented in mainstream dance companies, particularly in ballet. I was keen to empower and encourage them.

In April 2013, in London, I launched Artistry Youth Dance, which showcases and celebrates aspiring dancers of African and Caribbean descent aged between fourteen and nineteen years.

The company's dancers train in ballet, jazz, contemporary and dance forms of the African diaspora. The school enables young dancers to develop a sense of empowerment and the confidence to achieve success through the reinforcement that they are talented and important and have something of value to offer society.

The company has a core group of ten to twelve dancers who work with us over a one-year period, and we provide additional workshops for around 100 dancers per year. The students work with leading teachers, artists and choreographers.

It feels really positive to be able to give back, to contribute to the next generation of up-and-coming dancers. Working with young black dancers at Artistry Youth Dance always takes me back to the feeling I had when I went to the Ailey school for the first time. I enjoy encouraging these dancers to pursue their goals, dreams and ambitions, and to remind them to not be limited by the stereotypes that society projects, particularly regarding body shape and dance styles.

Many of the young people that have been part of the youth dance company have gone on to study at leading dance schools, colleges and universities. Some are now in West End shows and professional dance productions. It's been gratifying to see.

My upbringing in Sydney was integral in my journey as a dancer, a choreographer and now the founder of a black dance company. My family, friends and teachers provided me with support, which I can now pass on to my students.

There have of course been obstacles along the way. But in the end, it all hails back to that first memorable dance performance of mine, where my skirt began to unravel onstage. I learnt to keep my head high, be confident, smile and keep going. Find a way to overcome challenges, I tell my students. Keep on striving to achieve success.

Negro Speaks of Books

Inez Trambas

I was born in Hobart, on stolen Palawa land. My dad was from the Central African Republic, and my mum has a Greek background.

Hobart's small. There were lots of schools within walking distance of our home. I went to a private girls' school, but no matter what school you went to, everyone knew each other. The kids who went to other schools were my neighbours, and we all played together. I feel like that private–public school class divide, which is so obvious to me now in Melbourne, was not as extreme in the small city of Hobart.

There weren't many of people of colour in Hobart, and definitely not many Africans. Difference is something I was very conscious of when I was a kid. I was one of the only black kids at school, apart from my sister, which doesn't really count. In all the surrounding schools, there was one other black African-diaspora family, and one Aboriginal girl. It was just us, in this series of five or six schools. I definitely felt discomfort when I experienced racism, but I just accepted that that is how the world is.

I grew up listening to my Greek grandfather's stories about how he was treated when he immigrated to Tasmania. Those conversations taught me that difference is only as deep as the people around you make it. My grandfather never shied away from talking about how horrible his experiences were, but the Mediterranean community has pretty much assimilated in Hobart now. It's interesting talking to my mum, who has strong childhood memories of being othered in a way that was not about skin colour explicitly – because Greek people are still white – but was still about race and ethnicity, as when she was growing up, their culture was just teetering on an edge that Anglo-Australians then were not comfortable with.

In a lot of ways, my mum's experiences of childhood discrimination were similar to mine. It's fascinating to look at the timeline of when that shift occurred in Australian society. When did the white Australian community say, 'Greeks are fine, we love the wogs now'? It's a very complicated thing. I once heard it said that to be Australian is to hate the next wave of immigrants. That made me think about all the Greek and Italian people I know who are not very empathetic towards new generations of immigrants. It floors me, because they have stories like, 'They spat on me when I came here, I couldn't get a job, I stopped speaking my first language entirely because of all the racism,' and they're talking about really violent prejudice. On the other hand, they also say, 'These Africans aren't doing enough to fit in.' That doesn't make sense at all. Everyone's fighting for their right to be here, whatever that means, even though we're all on colonised land. Once people feel like they have that right, they will fight very hard to defend it, no matter how much their stories mirror those of the new migrants.

Despite its isolation from mainland Australia, my primary school did a pretty good job of having lots of different kinds of literature. I didn't read any books by African authors in primary school, but I was exposed to lots of South-East Asian authors. This was due largely to my fabulous school librarian. She always let me read in higher grades than I was supposed to. She would also always give me the new releases she got in. I often think about her, because she exposed me to the only brown characters

I knew. The only books with brown characters I read were because she put them directly into my hands and said, 'I've checked this out for you already.'

I had this teddy bear that I called Browney. Very creative name, I know. I used to write elaborate stories about him coming to life and going on adventures. In these tales he would journey across New Town, the suburb I lived in. He would catch the bus into town, and go to Myer and to the beach, but he would always get back to the house before I got home and discovered that he was secretly alive. The bear had brown hair, and I had brown hair. He had brown skin, and I had brown skin. I think creating a story about an anthropomorphised character was almost easier than creating an adventure story about a black girl who catches the bus to the beach in Hobart.

My mum really loves literature, and has inspired me in a lot of my reading. Her background is in science, but our house was always full of books and weird art things. She was very interested in the arts, even though it wasn't encouraged when she was young. You know how it is with immigrant families: 'Art doesn't bring in money. You're going to be a doctor, a scientist or an engineer. Did I leave my homeland for you to become an artist?!' My mum tried to work against that view, and to give us a sense that art is import-ant. She and my nanna used to say, 'You can have a toy or you can have a book. The toy you will get bored with in a few months. The book you won't get bored with. You choose.' It quickly became apparent to me that the book was the sounder investment.

My mum would write her favourite poems on contact paper and stick them up on the walls of our house as a form of dec-oration. When it came to decorating my room, I had to find some poems that I liked. I was six or seven at the time. My mum brought in all these different anthologies and poems that she liked. She suggested this poem 'Dream Variations', by African-American poet Langston Hughes, which ends with the iconic lines, 'Night coming tenderly / black like me'. Mum wrote it up in her beautiful handwriting and stuck it on my wall. I would come home every day and see that poem, and I would wake up and see it. The poem is Langston Hughes praising how beautiful it is to be black. He likens blackness to the beautiful night sky we all look up at. That was the origin of my black literature journey: it started there on my wall, when I was six.

I moved to Melbourne when I was in Year 7. I had never moved before: I'd lived in the one house in Hobart for my whole life. I knew everyone. Then I moved states, schools and houses. My mum was already living here, because she'd moved over to do her degree, and once she finished, my sister and I were able to move here and live with her. That was exciting because I hadn't lived with my mum for six years or so. It was very strange to move to a big city. When I lived in Hobart I was considered a city girl, but really Hobart was more like a town. Melbourne was definitely not like the city I grew up in.

I was on an academic scholarship to an 'elite girls' school' in the eastern suburbs. I had never seen people with so much wealth, and who were so unaware of how much wealth they had. We would go on an excursion, and the teachers would ask, 'Can a parent pick you up?' I would say, 'No, my mum can't pick me up. She's working. Can I please catch the tram home?' They would say, 'Can't your dad pick you up?' I would say, 'My mum is a single mum.' They would say, 'Well … can't your mum just leave work?' I would think, *What do you mean, leave work before she's finished her work? She's clocked on. I don't understand.* There were many little things like that, where they would expect me to be in certain circumstances because I was going to that school. At that time, not everyone knew I was on a scholarship. It would take me an hour and a half to get home from school because I used public transport, and we lived on the other side of the city. Other kids would say, 'What? Can't someone drive you?' Some of the kids I went to school with didn't know how to use public transport. I remember we went on one excursion to the city, and kids didn't know how to get home from there. That left me flabbergasted.

At high school, we read the modern Western classics. We always had to do an Australian text, which was usually something by a white author about what they thought growing up in the country was like, usually written by someone who lived in the city. We read those sorts of books, and maybe Charles Dickens or Jane Austen. If you were lucky, they might spice it up with George Orwell's *Nineteen Eighty-Four*. As I started reading more outside of school, reading the books I should have been reading all along, I became more frustrated with what I was reading at school. Reading books about feminism, and feminist struggles, was when I got really frustrated. I thought, *You've chosen this book because you feel like a certain class of young women will be able to relate to it and see parallels in their lives today, and be able to see how horrible it is that this was written in the nineteenth century and some things haven't changed, but I can't relate to this. This really doesn't seem that bad to me.* But I felt more frustrated for my peers, that they weren't going to read what I was reading outside of school, because I didn't think they would go and get it themselves. I felt sad for them, because school could be such an excellent place to do this kind of learning – learning about things that might be difficult to handle and dissect when reading about them by yourself. Like if you hadn't thought about the intersection of race and gender before, school could be such a great place to learn about those things. Kids would say, 'I read this at school, and I really liked it, so I checked out the author's other books, too.' If that's where your reading recommendations are primarily coming from – your curriculum – that makes me sad. Me, I was chilling, cos I had my city library card, and I knew that I could go and check out whatever I wanted, even while I was writing those student essays I had to write.

The first book I read that had a real impact on me was *Sister Outsider* by Audre Lorde. That was the first book where I thought, *Wow, this is the real reading experience. This must be what white people are so excited about! It's a good feeling! I get it now.* I'd always been an avid reader, but I would read whatever I was given, because I think all reading is valuable. If I'm reading something, I'm going to be interested in it, regardless of how much I disagree with it, because I like to be exposed to different ways of thinking. But when I read *Sister Outsider*, that was when I thought, *This is reading. This is capital-R reading!* I had not read a queer black female poet and nonfiction writer talking so frankly about everything her communities were experiencing. From there on, I started seeking out black writers almost exclusively. I would do all this googling. I would type in 'best black authors of the 21st century', and then try to find all of their books at the library or in the bookstore. Unfortunately, they're not very well stocked in Australia. Although it's nice to see it starting to change: I've seen a few bookstores in Melbourne in the last year alone close down to renovate, and when they open up again, they finally have more black authors! They needed to make the place nice so they could properly house these amazing books.

I also would go onto the Goodreads book-reviewing website to check things out. I love Goodreads, because there are reviews from ordinary people who have no stakes in the review. If I saw a review written in *The Guardian*, it would usually be written in some kind of pompous way where I didn't necessarily understand what it was saying. Goodreads would tell me the narrative clearly, and then tell me what I might like or dislike about the book. Then from Goodreads, I discovered the BookTube world: all the book reviewers on YouTube. They all had Instagram accounts, which led me to #Bookstagram world. They were all reviewing books in a very casual, accessible manner. They gave me the information I wanted to know, without the unnecessary embellishment that traditional book reviews seem to have. I was looking on social media for real human people and their thoughts about books. I found so many instances around the world of black people just reading black books, or queer African people reading queer African authors. These spaces were teaching me so much that I wasn't finding in the mainstream book media.

Still Nomads, the African-Australian arts collective in Melbourne, held a series of events in 2016 all about black literature. Every month, we would come together and talk about black authors, and watch YouTube videos of authors such as Toni Morrison. I was so grateful to find Still Nomads, and to be around other black people who were talking about the books they loved. It made me feel so validated. There is definitely a stereotype that black people can't or don't read.

So I was reading all of these books by writers of colour, particularly black authors, and I set a reading goal: 'I want to read thirty books a year' or something like that. I wanted to be accountable to that goal, and I have zero self-will, so I needed to be accountable to someone else. I started posting the books I read on Facebook, so my friends could see. When I saw my friends, they started saying, 'What are you reading now?' If I wasn't reading what I'd said I would be reading, I'd say, 'Damn, you caught me! Now I have to go home and read that.' Over time, my friends said I should just make my Facebook posts public, because everyone wanted to talk about what I was reading, and then in the comments section people would tell me what they thought of the book I had posted about, or what they were reading themselves. At first I said, 'No thanks, I don't want to go public. Public is scary.' But I'd been following all these Bookstagrammers and BookTubers, and I felt bad that I wasn't giving back to this community from which I was getting so much.

In August 2017, I started Negro Speaks of Books, my Instagram account. I started posting about everything I was reading. The name came about because I wanted to pay tribute to Langston Hughes, who wrote that first poem on my bedroom wall: the first black author I ever knew. Langston Hughes has a poem called 'The Negro Speaks of Rivers': 'My soul has grown deep like the rivers ... '

What has surprised me is how much people have engaged with it. I have these random conversations with people all over the world, whom I'm probably never going to meet. The diversity of the black people who follow me has been really important to me in my understanding of global blackness, and of colonialism. Getting recommendations back from people is incredible. People will comment and say, 'If you liked this book, you'll also like such-and-such.' People will sometimes send me photos of a book they've just bought because I've talked about it, and that's the best feeling. People will say, 'I read it, and it's the first time I felt represented!' or, 'I'd never heard of that author before.' That makes me so happy, because I became part of the online book community as I was having those exact same experiences in the spaces that other people had created.

I didn't grow up in the online space, or with social media. We didn't even have wi-fi a decade ago. When we got internet in the home, you couldn't be on the phone while the internet was on. People in our house would be yelling, 'Get off Club Penguin! Nanna needs to use the phone!' So even though I'm reviewing in the online space, my default method of finding books is still going to the bookstore or to the library. If I'm thinking of going, I have to allocate a minimum of an hour out of my day.

I also have a book club that I've been running since February 2018. Again, my friends urged me to do it. It's been fun to connect in that way as well. We've read predominantly black women. When I look at the success of online spaces like Glory Edim's Well-Read Black Girl, an online book club, and I see the other things she's done – things like a three-day festival she held for black women authors – I think that I would love to see something like that happen here in Australia. Although I acknowledge there has been some change in the way writers' festivals are run in Australia, and in the mix of authors on bookstore shelves, these are not changes we should settle for. I want to help open up this space, in whatever way I can.

I read for enjoyment and fun, and I read to find out about people's lives, to imagine how my life could be: it's not for any grander reason than that. But we do ourselves a great disservice, whoever we are, when we don't read widely. When you read work written by black authors and Indigenous authors worldwide – when you're reading at the intersection of so much, from people who have been underrepresented for 500+ years – you come to understand how the world works. They have all the stories to tell, and without them, every other story will be inaccurate.

Marhaba

Imam Nur Warsame

When war broke out in Somalia, people had to walk. The majority walked to the closest border, Kenya. Many people lost their lives; many women lost their children. We were lucky, my family: we didn't experience *qaxay*, the need to flee, because we'd left Somalia earlier, in late 1987 or early 1988, before the war. We went to Egypt. My mother took my brother and me, and my father followed later.

In Egypt, we did not have a permanent home. We were always on the move. This had both positives and negatives. For example, we attended several international schools, to study for the IGCSE: International General Certificate of Secondary Education. Children of ambassadors and so forth went to international schools, so we became aware of different cultures, especially Western cultures. Yet we were not allowed to go to the other kids' birthday parties. They were *haram*. So there was a cultural conflict from a young age. And we had no consistent friendships, as we were always on the move.

Alhamdulillah, I was lucky, in the sense that I always had the Qur'an with me. I remember reading the Qur'an out loud at the morning school assembly. One of the schools we went to was run by the Pakistani embassy in Cairo. They had an imam who would come for the *jummah khutbah*, the sermon, but I would lead the prayers. This helped me to connect with others in the school. For me, the Qur'an was a refuge: the place I always felt comfortable.

Alhamdulillah, it gave me a grounding.

Sheikh Muhammad Jibreel is a very famous Egyptian cleric. He used to come to the local mosque in Cairo. He would lead the prayer for fifteen days, sometimes reading a whole *juz* (the Qur'an is divided into thirty *juz*) in one night of Taraweeh prayer, which is performed during Ramadan. He had to have someone holding the Qur'an behind him, preferably a *hafiz* – someone who has memorised the Qur'an. So as early as nine or ten years old, I was leading the last fifteen days of Taraweeh with Muhammad Jibreel.

After leaving Egypt, we moved around a bit. I spent about two years in Italy, and just a bit over a year in Edmonton, Canada. Then we came to Australia.

I was a little bit overweight, and I loved KFC. There was halal KFC in Egypt. On the way to the airport to catch our flight, one of my uncles, who was driving us there, said, 'Nur, you know you're going all the way to Australia.'

'Yes.'

'You won't be happy.'

'Why?'

'In Australia they don't have KFC, they have KFK: Kentucky Fried Kangaroo.'

I believed him. When we landed, my brother and I looked around. *Where's this KFK?* we wondered. Then we passed a KFC in Brandon Park. We realised that our uncle had been lying to us.

During our first days in Australia, there was one thing I found especially strange. When I would walk around the neighbourhood with my mum, people would smile at us. I would say to Mum, 'Why? What are these people laughing at?' But I realised in time that they were just trying to be friendly. It was different from Egypt, and from what we had seen before, but alhamdulillah.

Speaking English helped us greatly, including in going to the shops. It was easy for us to slot into the community and feel part of it.

....

I still have the first Qur'an that I started memorising with. It's falling apart, but I carry it with me always. In the last half of Year 11, I was a school captain and the school imam. In my local area, I was already leading prayers: Taraweeh and so forth. It didn't matter where I was, I always had my Qur'an. The following year, Year 12, I was the school captain, the school imam and the imam of my local *musalla*, at Monash University. Towards the end of Year 12, I had about twenty *juz* of the Qur'an memorised.

After I finished school, my parents said, 'You have to go to university.' But I wasn't interested in that. My focus was finishing my memorisation of the last ten *juz*, to complete the Qur'an. I was trying to get into different places that specifically catered for Qur'an memorisation. I was looking to go to Pakistan or South Africa, but my father advised me to go back to Cairo, or to Madinah in Saudi. Instead, I found a contact who knew somebody in South Africa, in Darul Uloom. I sent a letter to ask the principal, who was also the owner of the school, if I could attend. I wrote, *Look, I'm a young man in Australia, and I've already finished my twenty* juz. *My parents want me to go to university, but I want to finish my last ten.* Soon after, I got a response: *You have been awarded a full scholarship.* So alhamdulillah, I went there, and I stayed one year, and I came back as a *hafiz*.

I returned around the end of 2001, soon after the September 11 attacks on the World Trade Center. I got a job at La Trobe University in Bendigo. You can imagine Bendigo in 2001: there was one train, to and from the city. In this climate of fear, I had a beard, and I used to wear my long *thobe*. Once, somebody vandalised my car on campus. The chancellor or the vice-chancellor – I can't remember his title – looked after me. He gave me a separate parking space. But even so, I didn't feel safe. I was supposed to stay there for the week, Monday to Friday, and return home only on weekends, but I couldn't stay longer than two or three days at a time. I had to come home. It wasn't an environment I was comfortable in.

My mum used to prepare food for me when I returned. She would say, 'My son, don't come home, just stay here.' But I had to go back.

My mother even visited me at work, just to reassure herself that everything was okay.

During that period, I was on a personal journey. I was having a personal struggle. I was in an environment where I could not talk about sex or sexuality. It was taboo, *haram*. There was this silence around desire and, as an LGBTQIA Muslim person, I didn't feel comfortable or safe to discuss my sexuality even with my family.

I kept quiet for many years. I passed as an imam. But being an imam added another layer of difficulty. I was dealing with people, including young people who were going through these same issues, but if you can't address your own sexuality, how can you address others' authentically?

Repressing your desires causes a level of trauma. That trauma generally leads to anger, which is either turned outwardly, resulting in violence against others, or inwardly, resulting in violence against the self. I experienced that. I attempted suicide.

It happened just after I separated from my wife, in 2006, which was also just after our daughter was born. I was hospitalised in the same Monash hospital she was born in. I had thought that maybe suicide would be easier than confronting my sexuality, but I didn't really want to die. They say about seventy-five per cent of people who attempt suicide don't want to succeed.

I remember my father saying, 'Get married again. One wife, no problem. Get another one.'

I wanted to find my independence, but that's very difficult for people in our community. Seeking independence is a rite of passage most individuals undergo. But often, our parents don't want to let go. From 2010 to about 2013, I was in a state of searching. I moved away from my family. I was on my own; it was like I was in the wilderness. I said, '*Ya rabi*, I am making a *hijra* (journey) to you now, wherever you take me.' I didn't want to go back to being the imam that I was previously, but I didn't know what shape the next chapter was going to take for me.

I prayed every night. I still do and, insha'allah, always will. But back then, I said, 'Allah, give me a sign, show me, open something for me.' Alhamdulillah, in November 2013, something changed. They say God works in mysterious ways.

I received a phone call from a school psychologist who was counselling a sixteen-year-old student in an Islamic school. The student felt like a boy trapped in a girl's body, transgender. Her parents had discovered that she was researching this online. The family sat her down for an intervention. They said, 'Forget Allah accepting your prayers. If you pray with these feelings, in fact, your prayers will be cursing you.' Imagine a sixteen-year-old being told that.

This school counsellor was not Muslim. She had found my details. 'Nur, I want to ask you a question,' she said when she called. 'I'm dealing with this new case in an Islamic school. It is just a theological question. The parents said this to their child. Is this true? Do you guys believe that?'

I said, 'Hell, no. We don't.'

That night, I didn't sleep. I was up all night, praying and praying.

There has been a vacuum in support services for LGBTQIA Muslims, I was thinking. That was what drove me to start something.

The next day, after a night of not sleeping, I came up with Marhaba, which roughly translates to 'welcome'. It was an idea for a Muslim prayer outreach group, an online community for Muslims who were questioning their sexual orientation or openly identified as a member of the LGBTQIA community.

It took that young person two weeks to feel comfortable enough to even get on the phone to speak to me. For two weeks, I was speaking to them through the counsellor. What families do to their own: the trauma is irreversible. I'm still in contact with that young person, who I'm pleased to say is doing well.

As of November 2018, it has been five years since I decided to extend this welcome, but it feels like yesterday. We don't have the concept of excommunication in Islam, as they do in the Catholic Church. Recently, I think a Catholic priest in the Vatican Council who decided to come out as gay was excommunicated. The church has that authority. But we don't have such a central authority figure. The excommunication happens in a different style. I call it the Muslim style. You slowly, slowly, stop receiving invitations to the mosques, the classes, the events. One sheikh in rural Victoria told me, 'Sheikh Nur, we heard of what you're doing. We support it, but we cannot support you publicly.'

Sometimes the threat is more overt. Last year, two men came to my door and threatened to kill me, after I'd appeared on the Melbourne-based LGBTQIA radio station JOY FM. They wanted me to stop talking about gay Muslims. But luckily

Victoria Police was very helpful and I am okay.

One of the most hurtful things was no longer being allowed to teach children that I had taught for some time – some I had spent more than ten years teaching the Qur'an; they had started their *elif ba*, alphabet, with me in Arabic. One was up to nine *juz* of the Qur'an when his father called me and said, 'Sheikh Nur, I heard about your work. I am sorry, we can't have you teaching our son anymore.' It was like someone had taken a dagger and pierced me in my heart. I had been teaching this kid for a decade.

I had thought of these consequences – it was not as though they hadn't occurred to me. I thought about them the whole night before I started Marhaba. I reflected on the different reactions and even threats that may result, targeted towards me and my family.

But I was prepared to live with these consequences. I wasn't willing to live with the realities of going back to being an imam in the same environment, where a sixteen-year-old could come into my *masjid* and I would not be able to advise them on the trauma they were facing in their house because I wasn't addressing my own sources of trauma. I wasn't being authentic to myself. I wasn't willing to live with facing a young person and not being able to tell them that they are okay, that there is nothing wrong with them. I couldn't do that.

I think it was Allah, subhanahu wa ta'ala, who gave me this strength. I believe with conviction that it came from Allah, because sometimes, when I look back, I think, *Far out. How did you do that?*

But I would do it all over again.

Around 2015, the second year of Marhaba, at various times I had people living in my one-bedroom apartment who had been exiled from their homes and communities – there were six or seven in total. I think either the third or fourth person had come to me homeless when a lesbian Muslim sister, a lawyer, said, 'Nur, there's this new position that has been announced under the Daniel Andrews government, and there's a woman who might be able to help you.'

I met Rowena Allen. She is the Victorian Commissioner for Gender and Sexuality, the only such commissioner in Australia. She had gone through the same issues that I was talking to her about in relation to LGBTQIA Muslims. Her family was from rural Victoria; I'm not sure whether they were Anglican or Uniting Church but, either way, they kicked her out.

Three to five months after my meeting with the commissioner, the Andrews government announced a $15 million Victorian Pride Centre to be built in St Kilda. But there was no provision for services to address the homelessness issue I spoke to the commissioner about. Instead, I was offered a prayer room. My response, when pressed on camera, was: 'Shove your prayer room.'

We talk about living in a multicultural society, but the same kind of treatment happens to LGBTQIA Indigenous communities, too. We are all forgotten, even though evidence shows that the level of homelessness for LGBTQIA people is actually increasing, not decreasing. Money is there, but the politicians channel it to suit their own agendas.

What was most troubling for me was the lack of support from the established LGBTQIA organisations. I went to the Victorian AIDS Council and the NSW AIDS Council. These were organisations that thirty to forty years ago came into existence to fill a vacuum in support services. But thirty to forty years later, they won't help us.

After the Orlando Pulse nightclub shooting in Florida in 2016, I spoke at Federation Square. It was the largest crowd

I had ever spoken to. What I found most heartwarming was not just the number of people there but the presence of several Somali Muslim girls in hijabs. They stopped me afterwards, as I left Federation Square to cross the road to St Paul's Cathedral. They said, 'Thank you very much, Sheikh Nur, for what you are doing. We are not LGBTQIA, but we are Muslim, and we support what you are doing.'

I will never forget that.

There is a shift happening in Australia – new spaces are being carved out around the world. There is a shift happening globally. Praise be to Allah, before and after. I hope it's a shift towards some more *rahma*, mercy, in our homes and in our hearts. There is great opportunity for healing to happen, if only we let it.

The Horse in the Room

Keenan MacWilliam

My parents adopted me straight from the Canadian hospital where I was born. They were on a long waiting list, and had a while to go before they would receive a baby. Then, out of nowhere, they got lucky. Another white couple were at the Toronto Women's College Hospital to pick up their new baby, and were disappointed when I was placed in their arms and they noticed my mop of curly black hair and my ethnic features. I was a healthy baby but I wasn't ... white. They no longer wanted me. My parents got a late-night call and, soon after, their first baby.

In early childhood, there wasn't much emphasis put on the fact that my origins are Guyanese. I grew up in a white neighbourhood where everyone always pretended that I was white. I have a light-ish complexion, which I think made it easier for them to pretend. My Zambian brother, who is also adopted, is much darker skinned than I am. I can't speak for his experience in our community, but I suspect that it was much more difficult for him.

I had mostly white friends and, more significantly, white parents. Parents who loved their children more than anything but sometimes missed the mark when it came to things beyond their experience. It was only later in life that I started to see that my parents' 'Love sees no colour' t-shirts were inadvertently erasing the identities of my brother and me.

Around 2001, a couple of months after my eleventh birthday, I moved all the way from Canada to Melbourne, for a full-time job. I was to play Carole Hanson in the hit television series *The Saddle Club*, based on the popular children's book series written by Bonnie Bryant. The plot follows a group of young girls who ride horses at the fictional Pine Hollow Stables. The job required me to smile a lot, and sometimes I'd sing and repeat words that others instructed me to say. I would do all these things while on horseback.

I still feel awkward when I see that name, Carole. I had to take a dive into the archives of my childhood career, playing a character who was at the time one of the few non-white girls on mainstream Australian television, to finally understand why.

My experiences in heading from Ottawa to Melbourne – from one mostly homogeneous environment to another – weren't necessarily dramatic, but there were subtle things that helped shape me subconsciously.

Like most eleven-year-olds, I was desperate to fit in, but fitting in was difficult for me. In a sea of Australian blue-eyed blondes, I couldn't help but stick out. I was the only frizzy-haired brown girl I saw while in the country, even if I didn't really recognise this at the time. Playing make-believe, when the cast and I pretended to be pop stars, I was always Scary Spice. I never had a Disney character to bond with, either. Personality-wise, I didn't mind standing out. People often remarked that I was sensitive, whatever that means. I cried a lot about little things. But appearance was another matter.

It's only looking back now that I can start to truly identify what it was like to be the only main character whose hair rarely fit under the riding helmet, or why I never felt my best leaving the make-up truck having been sprayed with a burnt orange hue. My stunt double was a blonde girl they'd paint brown and put a cheap curly wig on, and no one ever talked about it. It was more important for everyone around me to pretend that I was white than to acknowledge the horse in the room: my blackness. They made it seem like it wasn't a big deal, but it *was* a big deal.

It's become apparent to me, almost two decades later, that my job was more than pretending to look for missing horses at Pine Hollow Stables for twelve to fourteen hours a day. For some kids in Australia, I became some small alternative to Scary Spice. Kids who looked different from the majority had someone to watch after school – someone who, like them, didn't look like everybody else, but who also wasn't just defined by that physical difference.

When young-adult author Bonnie Bryant wrote the character of Carole Hanson, she wrote about a young girl who had a healthy relationship with her black father, wanted to be a veterinarian one day and would do anything for her two best friends. I remember reading for the role and immediately feeling a kinship with Carole: her love of animals, her belief in friendship, her sensitive and emotional approach. I remember, at eleven, feeling old; inside, I was a grown woman. Carole was like this, too: her lines were always the most grounded, the most reasonable, and showed a girl who was true to herself. She was an idealised version of me. Carole had depth, and she had empathy. She was probably the most intelligent character in the series (sorry, Stevie and Lisa).

After the show wrapped, I started auditioning for 'ALL ETHNICITIES WELCOME' roles on shows such as the popular Canadian high-school drama series *Degrassi*. Reading for the role of the cousin from 'the wrong side of the tracks', I'd be asked to speak with an 'urban' accent or to be less 'nice' in my delivery. I came to realise how rare the opportunity was to play a well-rounded character like Carole.

Throughout my early life I felt out of place, and not in an obvious way. The uneasiness was insidious, the kind of feeling that's hard to wrap your head around and almost impossible to distinguish when you're already going through puberty. I was young and didn't have a full grasp of my identity yet.

The time I spent in Australia as Carole Hanson, the purple-clad *Saddle Club* girl with a horse named Starlight, and the recognition I received for that role, was inadvertently the beginning of a lifelong journey of discovering myself. Seeing how strangers perceived me, worlds away from home, helped build my tapestry of understanding. It encouraged me to understand that I didn't need to fit the description that was placed upon me, and instead could define for myself who I was.

I regret ever ignoring the differences that make me who I am. These days, I love my blackness so intensely that sometimes it makes me resent the part of me that's white.

Being an adopted, biracial, gay woman means I've gone through life dealing with people telling me who I should be, versus figuring out who I want to be for myself. There has been loneliness and confusion in battling the highs and lows along that path. I'm still overcoming some of the prescriptions I've been assigned. But I think I'm getting somewhere.

Street Activism

Jafri Katagar Alexander X

I've got African names, I've got Muslim names and I've got nicknames. My African name is Tabu Ley. My mother used to love a Congolese singer named Tabu Ley. He was one of the greatest musicians of the Congo, and I was named after him. It's a bit hard for people to pronounce it here. My Muslim name is Jafari, but my nickname here in Australia is Jafri, because people find it very hard to pronounce the name Jafari. They kept pronouncing it wrongly, and that pissed me off. So I said, 'Just call me Jafri.'

I come from Uganda in East Africa. I grew up with a single mother. My mum and dad separated a long time ago. I saw my father about three times away from home, and then I heard he passed away, in 1997.

Growing up without a father didn't affect or bother me because my mother was my everything; she was both my mother and father. I have only one half-brother living in Africa, but I have many, many cousins.

I come from a Muslim background. My mother and father were Muslims. I have many uncles and aunties. My uncles have many children. It's acceptable for them to marry more than one woman; it's part of the culture where I come from.

My mother was a businesswoman. She travelled a lot from place to place. She used to take me with her, and sometimes leave me with other relatives. I lived in the Congo, I lived in Sudan,

I lived in Uganda, I lived in Kenya … I came to know all of my cousins, aunties and uncles.

My whole childhood, I never imagined I would ever come to Australia. I thought I would live in Africa for my whole life, with my mother. She loved me so much. She was like my god. She was the best mother in Africa. I always thought my mother would be around supporting me. She wanted me to go to the best schools, go to the best university, get a beautiful job, marry. She used to say with a smile, 'Look after me when I get old. Marry a good woman, so that she doesn't mistreat me.' Things like that. She always wanted the best for me.

The last time I saw my mother was in Kampala, the capital of Uganda. When I think about it, I feel like crying. I was in school studying there, and living in a hostel. I came to see her in the hotel where she was staying. She was about to go to South Sudan for work. I had a bad feeling about it. I was telling her, 'Don't go, don't go.' She said, 'I have to go. I have to get money to feed you, to pay your school fees, to pay for your clothing.' She said she had to go, for me and my brother. But I had a bad feeling. I didn't want her to. Sometimes when she would go it would take one or two months; it would take a long time. But she went. She went to South Sudan and the next thing I knew I was at school, and somebody called me, and said, 'Your mother has passed away.' It was 2003. I thought my mother was like God, and that she would always be around. So her death shocked me.

At the time my mother died, South Sudan was in a bad situation. She had fallen ill. There was no hospital. The plane flew out from there only a few times a week, so they were waiting for a plane to take her to Nairobi in Kenya for treatment, but it took too long, and she died waiting. My uncles went and got her body, and brought it back to Uganda for the funeral.

Everyone was waiting for me to arrive at the funeral. At an African funeral people cry really loudly: they wail. They were already crying when I arrived, but when they saw me, they started to wail even louder. When I saw the body, that was the first time I really believed she'd died. I cried for about four years, crying and crying for my mother. Right up until now, fifteen years later, I can't look at photographs of my mother, otherwise I will cry, so they are all hidden away.

My mother had been paying school fees for my brother and me. Compared to my cousins, I am one who has a lot of education. My aunties and uncles, they didn't care so much about education, so there was nobody who could keep me in school. I felt as if I should have been the one to die, and she should have stayed alive. I really felt that. She was such a wonderful person. I started to feel sick all the time, feeling a lot of pain in my chest, as if my heart was going to burst. My aunty sent me to the doctor, and the doctor said I needed to stop worrying about my mother, or it was going to do me serious harm.

My aunty was worried about me. I was sad all the time. The Australian government was taking migrants from Sudan and other parts of Africa. My aunty said she had a friend in Melbourne who went to Australia in 1999. She told him about me and said, 'Can you do something to help this boy, please? His mother is dead, his father is dead, he needs help badly.'

My aunty's friend proposed that I go and live in Australia. He sent some forms to Uganda. I had people help me with the forms, because I didn't want to make a mistake. I was happy, because I knew if I came to Australia I would have the chance to go to school, to go to university and find a good job and be able to fulfil my mother's dreams.

I put in the forms. It took about three months, and I was

issued a visa. Another aunty sent me money for the ticket. Everything I'd heard about Australia was positive. The night I flew into Melbourne there was an AFL game on, so from up in the sky I was seeing the bright lights of the MCG. There were so many lights, such bright lights. It was too much. As soon as I stepped out of the plane, I felt cold. It was as if they had put me inside a fridge! I thought, *When is this going to stop?!* It was the first time I had experienced winter. Where I come from, it doesn't get cold, like in Melbourne.

I waited at the airport for my aunt's friend to come pick me up but I think he was stuck in traffic. There was a woman watching me, waiting. I was there for a long time, and she offered to drop me to where I was going, because I had the address. She was about to take me, and then my aunty's friend arrived.

I knew that I was coming to a majority white country, so that didn't surprise me. As a child growing up in Africa, I saw a lot of white people who work with NGOs. Since childhood, I'd always loved seeing people who looked different from me. I would go up to them and talk to them. I'd ask, 'Hi, where have you come in from?' They'd say, 'Germany, Switzerland …' I used to be so happy talking to them, so when I came here, seeing many of them, I was happy.

I stayed with my aunty's friend in Endeavour Hills for about three months, and then I found accommodation in Noble Park. In Africa, people are more like family. Where I come from, we all know each other. Every person is known. We know who our neighbours are. But in Australia, most people don't know who their neighbours are. It's like you're on your own. That's one big difference I noticed about Australia. A few months after arriving in Australia, I went for a walk in the city. Everyone I saw was just staring at me like I was an alien from another planet. They were not smiling. I immediately felt something was not right.

As part of the program I was on then, if you came here as a refugee or on a humanitarian visa, you had to spend 500 hours or more learning English. My English was okay because I came from Uganda – Uganda was colonised by the British and English is their official language. My English was better than most of the people in the class. A lot of people, when they come to Australia, they want to work. For me, it was first about education. I wanted to be who my mother wanted me to be.

I did Year 12 at Dandenong TAFE for one year, and then I applied to Monash University. My results weren't good enough. They told me to apply for Monash College, and then I could get into Monash University from there. So after Monash College, I went into second year at Monash University, studying business and commerce. But unfortunately in 2013 I was discontinued from my studies by the university after I failed to pay my university tuition fee balance of $1385.90. I had no money, and struggled finding work. I was receiving Austudy but paid it all to the university to cover my tuition. This left me without any money to buy food or pay rent. I relied on food vouchers from the Monash Oakleigh Community centre to survive. I had a nice landlord who allowed me to stay in his house without paying rent. He told me not to pay rent if I didn't have the money.

I was on a payment plan but still I never had enough money to make all my payments on time. I begged the university to give me more time to pay my tuition but they refused. I was discontinued from my studies, and I was told I was no longer a Monash student.

I had already completed twenty-one units of my course. I had three units left to finish my degree. I was so devastated. During that time I also lost my grandmother, my grandfather and a cousin back in Uganda, and I couldn't go for their funerals due to lack of money.

I started volunteering at the Springvale Community Aid and Advice Bureau in south-east Melbourne. There, I came across many unemployed young people. I started conducting a youth unemployment campaign, whereby in November 2014 I wrote to every federal member of parliament about the problems affecting young people in Australia. In that same year, I was awarded a certificate of appreciation for my volunteer work by Clare O'Neil, the federal member for Hotham.

I had some serious dental problems. I was on the waiting list to see a dentist for more than three years. Then, finally, I was sent to a dental hospital in Melbourne. They took out about eight of my teeth. They took out a lot of my bottom teeth and left me with nothing there. Then, they inserted a fake bridge in my mouth, which caused me pain and discomfort. I was sent to go see another doctor in the same hospital to assess if I was suitable for implants.

When I saw this doctor, she asked me straightaway why I had come to see her. She started verbally attacking me. I was shocked. It was my first time meeting her. She treated me like someone who had done something wrong. I tried telling her that I had been sent so she could assess me for implants, but she wasn't listening to me. She wouldn't allow me to complete a sentence. Each time I tried to talk she interrupted me and shut me down.

I told her that I didn't come to the hospital to argue or upset her, but the more I talked, the angrier she got. I thought if I remained silent, she would calm down. When she saw that I wasn't talking anymore, she started to mock and ridicule me. She then yelled out sarcastically to her colleague in the next room, 'Hey, come talk to him – he doesn't understand English!' She said that she would record that I refused treatment at the hospital. She said to me, 'You're black; you don't understand.' I left the hospital with tears in my eyes. On my way back home while in the tram, I felt like leaving Australia and going back to Africa.

A day after the hospital incident, I complained on the hospital's website about the way I was treated, but received no response. I reported the incident to the local police but the police said they couldn't arrest the doctor unless I provided video evidence, which I didn't have. I was too poor to afford a lawyer.

I took my case to the Health Services Commissioner. The department contacted the dental hospital regarding my complaint, but the hospital completely denied any wrongdoing. I decided to take my case to the Australian Human Rights Commission, but they said they couldn't look at the case, because it was already looked into by the Health Services Commissioner.

I came up with the idea of self-protest, because there was nobody helping me. I was not an activist and had never done any activism before that.

I informed the police that I was going to protest, and they wished me good luck.

I stopped doing my volunteer work and started protesting in front of the dental hospital with two signs. One sign said, 'STOP RACISM NOW' and the second sign said, 'I WAS MIS-TREATED & HARASSED IN THIS HOSPITAL'.

In my first week of protesting nothing happened, but in my second week of protesting, the executive director of the hospital and another member of staff came out and apologised to me on the street on behalf of the hospital, saying they were very sorry for what I had experienced. I told them that I was happy they were finally apologising, but I asked for an apology letter. I suggested they train their staff in how to deal with patients of different cultures or backgrounds. They said they would order the doctor who mistreated me to write me an apology letter. About a week later, I received an apology letter from the hospital that didn't match up with the personal apology that I received on the street. They were apologising, but not admitting fault. I never received an apology from the doctor who mistreated me.

In response to my request for the hospital to train staff in how to deal with patients of different cultures or backgrounds, the apology letter said they had amended their current cultural-awareness training to include sessions for clinical staff when communicating with patients chair-side during treatment. I haven't seen any evidence of what they've done.

It's been many years now, and I've still been left with no teeth on the bottom, and nothing has been done about it. It's very hard for me to eat a lot of things. I can't bite an apple. I can't eat popcorn. Racism has affected me physically, and it still affects me physically every day.

From the hospital, I moved over to Flinders Street. I chose Flinders Street because it's the heart of Melbourne. There, I turned my hospital protest into a general anti-racism campaign. I stood right outside Flinders Street Station, every day, with my 'STOP RACISM NOW' sign. I stood there not just because of what happened to me, but because even though African-Australians have citizenship rights, we are second-class citizens. When they talk about us, they still always say 'refugee'. We are treated like outsiders, despite some of us being born in this country. People think we're in gangs; that's what the media tells them. I hate all violence. I have never been violent one day in my life. If someone who looks like me commits a crime, it's all over the newspapers and on television. Then you will hear some people calling for deportation. It's unfair, blaming the majority for the actions of a few. This negative media coverage is driven by racism, and media outlets that want to sell papers, and politicians who want to score political points.

African-Australians face various forms of discrimination. Employers sometimes won't hire you because you are black or dark-skinned, or because you look or sound different, or because of the foreign name on your resume. People like me can take longer to find work, and as a result we may have lower incomes.

It can also take longer for someone like me to find a house to rent or buy. Some landlords and real estate agents are prejudiced, and they won't rent or sell their houses to black people.

When I go out to the shops to buy something, they look at me as if I am going to steal something. They watch me on the camera.

When you are black, you are easily stopped and searched by some police officers. When you are black, you look like a suspect, they stop you, they search your car and they find nothing, then they let you go. When you ask why, they say it's a routine check.

This is why I continue to campaign.

People react differently when they see me standing in the busy street with my signs. I have many times been called a 'black dog', 'black cat', 'nigger' and so on. I have also been told, 'Go back to Africa,' asked, 'If you don't like it here, then why did you come here?' and so on. I have been attacked and pepper-sprayed by the police.

Not all is negative, though. I also get some positive reactions from people. There are many people who support my anti-racism campaign and are happy to see me standing on the streets with the 'STOP RACISM NOW' sign. Sometimes white people show me pictures of themselves with their mixed-race children, or photos of their black partners and friends. Sometimes people hug me. Sometimes people walking past shake my hand, or stand with me for a while, or say thank you. Some people tell me things such as, 'You are welcome here,' 'We need more people like you in Australia,' 'Keep up the fight,' and so on. Some people give me flowers. Some police officers give me water in the hot summer, to keep me cool. There are also some police officers who tell me that if other officers are disturbing me, I should let them know. The positive reactions from people give me strength and courage to keep fighting and raising awareness about racism. Not every person is bad or racist. I don't say Australia is a racist country, but I say racism is a problem in Australia.

People started to get to know me, from standing there in the middle of the city with the 'STOP RACISM NOW' sign, but also because I attended a lot of anti-racism rallies. There was a refugee and anti-racism activist, Margaret Sinclair, from the Refugee Action Collective, whom I met at a protest at Flinders Street. She said she was meeting up with MP Jason Wood, the federal member for La Trobe, who was heading a parliamentary inquiry into migration settlement outcomes. She asked me to come with her to the meeting because I knew a lot about issues to do with the African-Australian community. I went to the meeting and as soon as I got home, Margaret contacted me and said Jason Wood wanted me to work for him, on a program to try to identify the barriers to African-Australian youth getting employment and to assist them.

When I went to work for him in his office, he asked me, 'Why aren't you in school?'

I tried to explain to him what had happened, that I had only three units to complete but my enrolment was discountinued due to late fees.

Jason contacted Monash University. In the beginning, the university spoke through their lawyers, but later on they relaxed.

Monash sent me an offer. I accepted the offer and I was given a new course, Bachelor of Business Administration, as my previous course was no longer available.

I asked the university to consider changing their procedures and policies so students from disadvantaged backgrounds wouldn't be forced out of or discontinued from their studies for not having enough money to pay their tuition on time. They replied saying they had put measures in place to prevent my situation being repeated, and increased support for refugee and asylum-seeker students.

Jason Wood is a Liberal politician. I am not affiliated with any political party, and my work with him was purely for my community. But other activists were saying, 'Don't talk to these people, these are not good people,' 'They are racists,' 'They are anti-Muslim,' 'They are anti-refugee.' Jason Wood is not a racist but a nice man. Protesting at Flinders Street, I speak to everyone unless they are aggressive or abusive. I see everyone as brother or sister. You can't change society if you avoid some people.

Just stick with love, that's my philosophy. Love is the only force capable of transforming an enemy into a friend. Hatred is a great burden to bear.

DHAQAN
CELIS

Dhaqan Celis

Magan Magan

I think I smell of war.
Of smoke and strange men
and calling cards.

I am originally from Somalia but was born in Yemen. After leaving Yemen, my family moved to Malta for a few years before migrating to Australia in 1991. My parents couldn't go back to Somalia because the civil war had broken out as they were moving from one country to the other. As a result, my parents had no contact with their families for years. My siblings and I were born in different countries: my older sister and brother were born in Saudi Arabia; my younger brother was born in Malta.

From the age of three, I remember carrying a heavy load of life – a sense of sadness, a strong feeling of being unsettled. Once we were granted permission to come to Australia, I remember my mother telling me that we'd made it. We were going to a different country that was peaceful, and we were going to build new lives – everything was going to change.

But when we came to Australia, that feeling didn't leave me. I still didn't feel settled. On our first drive to our first home, in Maribyrnong, I remember we were in a white van. I was right next to my mother. She had her hair out, and looked incredibly happy. She was wearing a brown velvet dress and a matching cropped jacket. I remember her asking me if I wanted to eat an apple she had in her bag. I said yes. For some reason, I didn't want to eat the apple skin. So she peeled the skin and gave me the flesh to eat. This mundane, uninteresting memory has stayed with me my entire life. Perhaps the apple, shed of its skin, represented what it would mean to become Australian.

Near our first home was a gated landscape where goats and cows were herded. My mother would tell me stories about when she was a little girl, in the countryside near a small town called Dila, located in northern Somalia, herding sheep. But we lived in walking distance from Highpoint Shopping Centre, in the heart of Maribyrnong.

When I was about seven, my mother bought both my younger brother and me a bicycle. We didn't know how to ride, so my mother and my sister taught us. They spent weeks practising with us, encouraging us to persist – it was done with so much love. Around the time I mastered riding that bike was when two white kids who lived in the same high-rise as we did told us 'niggers' to go back to where we came from.

In 1997, I was ten. It was the year I found out that 2Pac and I shared a birthday. My older sister was a huge 2Pac fan, and she is the reason '90s hip-hop played a role in my childhood. I wanted to be like 2Pac, except I did not want to be involved with drugs and violence. Instead, I was in awe of his energy and artistry. I remember falling in love with the music video to his track 'California Love', featuring Dr Dre. The costumes, the setting and 2Pac's lyrical flow were captivating. I also loved that he was considered short, as I had always been a small kid. My sister's obsession with him confirmed how cool he was; in my ten-year-old mind, my older sister had life figured out.

My mother jumped on this familial love of 2Pac when my sister showed her the song he wrote for his mother. In the Somali culture, parents are meant to be worshipped. Children are often seen as extensions of their parents. Before that song, 2Pac's music was 'too provocative', according to my mother. But whenever he was mentioned afterwards, my mother would always comment how beautiful it was that he wrote a song for his mother.

I never understood parents who raved on about their 'awesome' parenting. I remember once telling my mother to let me be the judge of our relationship when I was an adult. She scolded me: 'You kids are so spoilt in this country. I was obedient to my parents back home.' There is this poetic verse in the Qur'an that my mother would use to drone into us the importance of mothers: 'Heaven lies underneath the feet of your mother.'

Later that year, American pop-rock band Hanson released their lead single, 'MMMBop', from their album *Middle of Nowhere*.

I remember what seeing them did for me. It did for me something that 2Pac couldn't. I saw boys expressing an alternative form of boyhood that I desperately wanted. (That is, after I learnt they were actually boys.) They had perfectly long blond hair. They had high-pitched voices and sang songs that appealed to one's emotions.

There were two other boys at school who were also fans of Hanson, both white. One lunchtime, we decided to play Hanson. In deciding who was going to play who – Isaac, Taylor or Zac – we all revealed which Hanson brother was our favourite. I insisted on being Taylor, my favourite, because, like me, he was in the middle of two brothers. Both boys looked at me, confused, and asked how I could be Taylor when I looked nothing like him. I didn't care. I told them it didn't matter – this game was made up anyway. And I related to Taylor the most.

Amidst crying babies
and old men with orange beards
I am standing in a long line
swollen with anxiety
facing,
a faceless white woman
sitting at the desk behind a wall of glass
who says please and thank you.

Back in 1999, in my twelve-year-old mind, I felt we had been in Australia for a long time. Somalis use this term, *dhaqan celis*. *Dhaqan* means 'culture', and *celis* means 'return'. It is used to describe Somali kids who have somehow lost their culture or have failed to carry their culture, kids who need to return 'home' to align themselves with who they are.

My mother felt the gap between herself and her children more vividly as the years went on. Her dream for a better life in Australia began to feel bittersweet. My mother's solution to this was for us to experience some good old *dhaqan celis*. At the end of 1999, she uprooted us all to Somalia to learn about our culture.

If she needs me to, I can grow new teeth
that glisten like hers in the light
when she is speaking:
'It is important you fill in this form.'
First name: Running. Middle name: From
Surname: Bullets. Country of birth: Dust.
My city has become a wet passport.
When I look back I see women
pushing their babies underneath fences.

When we first arrived in Somalia, we stayed with my mother's cousin. Our ride to his house was interesting. We drove past plenty of half-blown-up buildings. I also saw many trees that looked exactly like the trees in *The Lion King*. I was reminded of the images of Somalia that the West focuses on: a country ruined by war.

After two years of *dhaqan celis*, we returned to Australia. It was late 2001, and I was fourteen. My voice was deeper, and my Somali was almost perfect. I got reacquainted with the Somali kids I grew up with. We sat on the Flemington Park oval and I told them all about camel milk, and how refreshing Somali music was. I said this in Somali, sitting on the same oval I had learnt to ride a bike on years earlier.

Growing up African in Australia has always felt like a giant negotiation. It has always felt like war. The need to know who I am in this desperate way has been a long battle.

When I was in Year 9 back in 2002, I remember telling my sister that the new school that Mum had enrolled me in looked very much like the '90s teen show *Heartbreak High*. I remember how excited I was to explore life the way the teens in that show did. The way they developed friendships and managed the stresses of relationships.

In that same year, the film *Black Hawk Down* was released. It was set in 1993, when the United States sent special forces into Somalia to save the nation from its horrors. It felt very strange having white Australia reference *Black Hawk Down* in its attempt to know me.

Suddenly, in this hypervisibility I found myself in a battle I hadn't had the chance to think about. With all its intensity, the world kept on asking me:

So what are you going to do
fold like a piece of paper
Sleep until your gums start bleeding
Turn your teeth into nameless refugees
Drowning

Just like that, I became a plastic boat in the sea, trying to cross the Indian Ocean.

Sam

Faustina Agolley

Mum always finds it hard to talk about him.

One day, around age five, I come home from school and ask her why I don't have a father. She isn't prepared to answer at the time, yet she's been expecting this question for a while. The next day at work, she calls a friend in tears, trying to find ways to broach the subject with me.

As I get older, I talk about him factually.

My father passed away from a car accident in London when I was a child. Never 'my dad'. It seemed too casual. *Father.*

People ask more. I tell them other stray facts I've learnt from hearing Mum speak of him in public. Facts that make no sense to me.

How old were you?

Seven weeks old.

Oh my god, you weren't a child, you were a baby. How old was he?

In his thirties.

That's so terrible. Your poor mother. And her?

Thirty.

The only other facts I know until I'm a teenager are that his name was Samuel and that he was from Ghana. I learn to say that Ghana is in West Africa, for people who don't know where Ghana is, or think Africa is a country. I also explain this to make a point to those confused by the sight of a Chinese woman with a black child. *Yes, this beautiful Chinese woman is my birth mother.*

Heads turn when my brother and I walk into a Chinese restaurant with our family for yum cha on weekends.

I grow up knowing his absence, instead of his stories. Random consequences follow his passing. I am pulled out of class to sit with an apparent counsellor, who asks me to talk and draw about my feelings. Mum has to juggle three jobs. My brother gets into fights at school. He runs away from our house in Clayton to my grandparents' home nearby. The second time he runs away, Mum makes the decision to move us all under their roof. It is all because of my father. My father, who passed away when I was a baby.

And your mum never remarried?

No.

She's so strong.

If I ask Mum a question about my father, she usually says that she can't remember the answer. If I am persistent, her voice quivers, a long silence follows and her soft brown eyes turn to anguish. Tears roll down her gentle face. In these moments I know I've gone too far. Asking questions, being curious, wanting to know anything beyond the violent, bleak facts of my father's death causes unattended trauma to the only parent I know and love. So I learn not to ask.

And yet, the trauma still looms between the three of us: trauma is conflated with a man who had a full life. A life I want to know about. But asking about it stuns Mum into a bereaved silence, the news of his death makes strangers horrified. I am lost.

TELEVISION

I spend a great deal of the early years of high school faking being sick so I can stay at home and watch *The Oprah Winfrey Show*.

I know the usual rhythm of the morning and the exact time to hijack it. Our rooster trumpets to punctuate the arrival of dawn and, although I always expect it, the sound makes me chuckle every time. I hear the familial tones of Kung Kung and Mama saying their twice-daily rosary, the smell of rice cooking, Mum quietly slipping out for another shift in the oncology ward at Moorabbin Hospital, and my brother leaving for a day of lectures and lab study at Monash University. Then, alas! My imagined sickness strikes, and I helplessly remain in bed.

Kung Kung observes me as he walks past my room. Then my grandmother, Mama, comes in.

'Ah-Mei, Ah-Mei, school now.'

'Mama, I'm sick.'

I cover my face with my doona. The sheets shield any evidence of me breaking character.

I hear Kung Kung, in his dulcet tones, inform Sacred Heart's secretary that I won't be in school that day. Once the phone hits the receiver, I feel free. There's a quiet celebration beneath my sheets, before I settle quickly back into the mysterious illness that has supposedly befallen my long-limbed, now-fragile body. The sickness conveniently remains until the day shifts closer and closer to Oprah's time on screen. Moments before Oprah's show begins, I am miraculously healed.

Besides my brother and the South African Perez family down the road, television is the portal to my black collective experience. My people are Will Smith and the Banks family who live in a town called Bel-Air. The sisters I party with are Lauryn Hill, Missy Elliott, TLC, Alicia Keys and Destiny's Child, who show up reliably every weekend, on *Video Hits*.

They all make me feel special and part of something bigger. But there's something else about Oprah. Oprah is our matriarch.

She radiates on screen. A full hour with Oprah is worth trading a day of school for. In a world of trashy, once-a-dog-always-a-dog television talk shows, she teaches me how to be a better woman in the world. Her audience screams with joy at the sight of her, and I feel their exhalation all the way from Chicago to Clayton.

'I'm going to work for you one day,' I say to Oprah, on the television screen. The words fall out of my mouth and I don't know why. All I know is that the pull is strong.

Boxes

Springvale is different from most suburbs in Melbourne. It's a home away from home for people from Malaysia, Vietnam, China, Indonesia and many other places. The main streets are lined with storefronts signed with bold fire-engine red and gold Asian writing. Roast duck and crispy pork hang in restaurant windows.

Most weekends of my teenage years are spent following Mum to stock up on groceries we can't buy elsewhere. We collect a lotto ticket from the newsagent adorned with Maneki Neko cats waving their motorised paws for good luck, and then I get to eat my favourite food: steamed and baked *charsiew baos*, a *banh mi* loaded with extra shredded pickled carrot, and coconut-filled *kweh*. If Aunty Rose is in town from Malaysia, we visit her too.

Mum and Aunty speak in part Fouzhou and part English over tea and treats. I zone out of the conversations and walk around Aunty's backyard. One weekend I look inside her garage. It is full of boxes. I notice a pile with my surname on them. *AGOLLEY* in large print gives me permission to open them at once. I break the seal on the box closest to me and release a burst of mildew. I look inside; I pull out vinyl records. The Supremes, The Beatles, Dionne Warwick. On closer inspection, handwritten on each of these records, in blue or black ballpoint pen, is the name *SAMMY*. The ends of the S's curl more elaborately than most handwriting I've seen, and the A's, the double M's and the Y's look like they were written with striking speed: their strokes sharp and confident.

The hairs on my arms stand tall. I pick up the box, race inside Aunty's home and interrupt their conversation. My discovery is more important.

I show Mum the records. A shock of recognition dawns upon her face. She professes forgetting that she brought any of his belongings to Australia. Unlike a lot of the times she has told me she can't remember, I believe her.

Aunty Rose isn't surprised, and says they've sat in her garage the whole time. A whole thirteen years.

Huh.

We all head back to the garage to inspect the other boxes. There are photographs. I lay my eyes on my father for the first time. He's tall and handsome, with a 1000-watt incandescent smile. No wonder Mum fell in love with him. Almost every photo seems to capture an intangible quality. He's the life of the party: he brings a presence, a magnetism. He looks like he *knows* it.

There are photos of them from when they were dating. Young love. His arms around Mum by their Mini Cooper. In another photo he's smartly dressed in a brown suit, dancing among England's snow. In the summer months, he wears flared denim jeans, and yellow t-shirts that hug his strong, lean physique.

A flood of memories come to Mum. She begins to tell me stories. She refers to him endearingly as 'Sam' or 'your dad'. I've never heard Mum speak like this before. They met when Mum was studying to be a nurse. My father was already a nurse, and specialised in psychiatry. Mum tells me about one of their first dates. He took her to see the Temptations. He was Mum's first and only partner.

I find a diploma in social studies. He wanted to work for the World Health Organization. They had a beautiful wedding, with twenty friends at best, because neither set of parents could afford the tickets to fly to London. And they had dreams to move to Australia, my mother and father, I'm told.

I find precisely ten photos taken at my birth. A lot of them are taken by my brother, who was seven years old at the time, and have been shot inaccurately. You can see the tops of our parents' heads and a lot of wall and ceiling. Despite these shoddy attempts, there's a photo of my father and me. He's holding me and, unlike in the many other photos I see of him, he looks exhausted. I'm at the bottom of the photo, which is mouldy from water damage. There is just the one photo of us together, and it's disfigured by nature, which gives me the chills. But it will do.

SOUND

The boxes moved to Mum's townhouse the day we left Aunty's.

I ask Mum to buy a record player. I wipe the mould off the vinyl discs. I feel that the first record I play is important, like ushering in my father's soul to dance with me. Diana Ross and the Supremes seems appropriate. I place the needle on the vinyl, and the machine picks up speed and plays 'Stop In the Name of Love'.

I've heard this song many times before, but the vinyl makes the song sound warmer, like I've returned home to its original precious form. It's an awakening. Although the song is familiar to me, the sound is astonishingly new. It's as if my father, posthumously and in spirit, is revealing something different about our shared love of music. Unlike previous times, I hear every instrument, every intention, and the orchestration is perfectly mixed. It's clear that all the times I heard this song before were counterfeits. I thank Mum for keeping the records. His once-forgotten possessions are ours again, and this man feels even more real to me.

I try to call him 'Dad'. It sounds weird coming out of my mouth, but I keep trying now and again.

After some months, Mum and I make time to tend to the boxes again. She excitedly breaks the seal of one of them in her living room. A smaller box is inside. Mum is intrigued and opens it. There's an envelope that reveals a macabre discovery. Someone took photos at Dad's funeral. His dark coffin is closed, but there's a window that reveals his face. Markings from the car accident. He's scratched and wounded. He's there but he isn't: as if his essence left his body a long time ago.

I look for Mum's reaction. She's breathless. There's the usual silence, but then, this time, Mum bellows out a guttural, harrowing cry. I've never heard Mum cry like this before. It rams into my body and the trauma fills every part of me, and I cry at her distress and mine. But I feel guilty for my tears.

In another photo are the solemn faces of men and women on the church steps. My mum stands outside; her eyes are vacant. My brother's hands are on the hearse's window. He peers in to see the coffin ... Dad ... before the hearse pulls away.

ALIZATA MAHAMA

The phone rings at Kung Kung and Mama's house. It's for Mum. On the other end of the line is Dad's sister, Aunty Alima. She tells Mum she travelled from Ghana to London, and arrived at our doorstep to find out from our neighbour that we moved to Australia over a decade ago.

I don't know what else is exchanged on the phone call, but it's enough for Mum to take money off the mortgage for our first overseas trip.

'It's important you know your dad's side,' she says to my brother and me.

We land in Ghana at night. When the plane door opens, I'm almost bowled over by the hot tropical air. We walk out of the airport, and it's so different from a crowd in Melbourne: all the faces we see are black as midnight. Alima's husband, Adam, emerges from the crowd. He's our host for the two-week trip, as Alima is still in London.

Adam takes us to see our grandmother for the first time. Mum hasn't even met her before. Her name is Alizata Mahama. She's a lot taller than my Chinese grandmother, and there's a peaceful reverence about her. Language is a barrier between us all: she speaks in Ga, and Adam needs to translate.

She blesses Allah for this moment, and then gently directs her attention to my brother and me. Adam translates: 'She says you look just like your father.'

We already knew this in some way, but with him being gone for so long it feels ephemeral. Her words ground us in a sense of home: in our dad, in her and in Ghana.

We're all moved by this moment, and by all the circumstances over the years that finally culminated in us being together.

Grandma makes *fufu* for us for our first night in Accra. I sit over the two bowls. One looks like spicy curry; the other, the *fufu* itself, looks like raw dough. It smells sour. I'm told it's cassava and plantain. We're taught to pick the dough with our fingers and dip it into the soup. I pick the dough, and it's soft and sticky. I dip it in the curry and place it in my mouth. It's the spiciest soup I've ever tasted, and the fermented smell of the *fufu* singes my nose. I've been hungry for a couple of hours now, but I can't stomach this. I feel awful for not liking Grandma's dish. Word gets back to Grandma that the dish is too spicy for me. The next day, Grandma arrives from the market holding a live chicken and makes a milder stew. It's custom to slay a live animal for the arrival of family. These gestures, the cooking, all imbued with love, are akin to my life in Australia with my Kung Kung and Mama. I couldn't be prouder of my dual roots.

Throughout our trip everyone we encounter wants to know our name, and once they hear we are Agolley there's a recognition. 'Ah, you are from the north!'

We're of the Bawku people, and our tribe is Kusasi. Hearing that I am from a lineage of an actual tribe makes me feel like the coolest kid on the planet. Bawku runs close to the border of Burkina Faso and Togo. We consider going there, but we're told it's much hotter than Accra, and the fact that I've fainted a couple of times already quickly makes that decision.

Slave ports still sit on Ghana's coastline. I stand on the history that binds us all globally, the violent colonialism. I see shackles, and cannons that point out to a turbulent sea. There's a sign above a door that says *POINT OF NO RETURN*. I stand under the sign and touch the door frame. I ruminate over the thousands of lives that were forced through there, a shared global black history, and a past that cannot be undone.

I find out that my dad had a brother named Peter Agolley. One day, at age sixteen, Peter went missing walking home from school. He never returned home. He was likely taken for modern slavery, which was common at the time, and still common today.

Throughout my grandmother's life she would ask, 'Will I see my son before I die?'

My time in Ghana puts a fire in me. I come back to Australia a changed young woman. Knowing that I have learning difficulties, I read every prescribed textbook and novel in the summer. Then Year 10 commences, and I sit in front of all my classes, ready to make the most of what I've got.

Video Hits

The discovery of my father's records; skipping school to watch Oprah Winfrey; my love of black music; my newfound confidence and work ethic – all of these memories collide when, years later, while studying at two universities, I land my dream job hosting *Video Hits* at Channel 10.

My work doesn't feel like work at all. Most of it is self-directed research in an office, in front of a computer with access to a vast archive of music videos. The payoff is the privilege of sitting opposite artists that have soundtracked the lives of millions of people – from emerging artists of the time, like Florence Welch and Calvin Harris, to living legends such as Ice Cube, Big Boi, Jack White and Green Day, to idols in the making, like Bruno Mars, Rihanna and Adele. I sneak my dog, Bo, into the fancy hotel room with Rihanna. I host Adele's first Australian television interview from a beautiful hotel in Soho, London. Adele picks up my guitar and plays 'Crazy for You'. Then she names my guitar Bruce. I get to meet some of my sisters from watching *Video Hits* in my high-school days. I dance with Kelly Rowland in downtown Los Angeles; I interview Alicia Keys backstage at Homebush Stadium. 'You ... I like you,' Keys says. 'You did a great job!'

I'm sure all of this would've made Dad proud. I'm sure he would've been pinching himself with me: life in Australia, a place he wanted to live, and a daughter with an education, the opportunity to travel and living her full life.

I am his legacy, and I hope to do him proud.

Diasporan Processing

Effie Nkrumah

PAGEWOOD (1988–1992)

My earliest memories of Pagewood, a suburb of southern Sydney, include eating gummy bears from the corner shop and collecting bottle caps with my dad, which we turned into fun toys with coloured thread. There was the Crystal truck that brought us awesome flavoured fizzy drinks while *Saturday Disney* was on: *DuckTales* and *Chip 'n' Dale: Rescue Rangers*. The sun shone through the white venetian blinds in that flat. I longed for days that would never come: where I would draw and mail my colourful, slightly lopsided drawing of Winnie the Pooh that the presenters of *Saturday Disney* would show during the episode.

....

'Mum, what are you saying?'
  'We are speaking Fante, Eff.'
  'We speak Fanta?'
  Laughter.

....

I started school in Pagewood. The emblem on my Pagewood Primary School uniform was Captain Cook's *Endeavour*. I should have understood then where we really were – what kind of country we lived in – but I didn't. On my first day of school, I cried.

It was mostly because I saw other kids crying, so I thought why not join in? I was the only black child in the school, the only child of Ghanaian descent.

MARRICKVILLE (1993–1995)

By the time my brother was born and my sister was on the way, we had moved to an old house next to the Church of Christ on Illawarra Road, in Marrickville. What a concentration of culture and experience that period was.

Every Saturday night we would go to a place called Fellowship in Newtown. It wasn't too far from a painted map of Africa that we drove past; I still didn't understand where we were, that this was Australia. We would meet and sing songs, Daddy would play the guitar, Mummy would sing, and I would get to see Aunty Chinwe and play with my friends Osas and Gifty and look at the weird white lady with long brown hair that fell everywhere. We would giggle at her and tell stories about how she was a witch. I saw her walking out of Newtown Station one night, I'd say, when we were driving to Fellowship, and she was wearing a black flowy dress, white pointed shoes and a tall, pointed black hat.

....

'Oh my god, she's so cute! What's her name?'

'Adjoa. It means "girl born on Monday".'

'Wow! Where are you from?'

'Ghana, West Africa.'

'Wow! So do you speak African at home?'

'There is no such thing as African. There are more than fifty languages in Ghana alone.'

On my first day at Marrickville West Public School a redheaded girl said I had nits because I was black. I didn't. I didn't even know what nits were.

There was only one white boy in my class and he never came to school. In Year 2, a Chinese girl called Michelle punched me. I was so mad I punched her back, and she cried. The substitute teacher made me sit on the floor at the back of the class. No questions were asked.

As I grew, I longed for a chance to be noticed. My dream was to become an actress, but I couldn't locate the way through to my dream. I was outspoken and funny, always considered one of the boys. I wasn't, or didn't consider myself, pretty.

When I was about seven years old, my parents took me to classes held by the Sydney Youth Theatre in Marrickville. The other kids and I were asked to sit in a circle. There was a male teacher, and he asked me to stand up, I did, thinking that I was going to improvise something. Instead, he asked me to follow him out of the room. He pointed at a dustpan and broom and asked me to sweep the room. I was confused, and gave him a questioning look. To this day, my memory ends there – I don't know if I swept like a servant girl or if he realised with shame that I was a confident child of educated people who taught me to value who I am.

Reservoir Road, Blacktown (1996–2001)

One evening, Daddy told us we were driving to Blacktown. It was so far from Marrickville. I asked Daddy if it was always night in Blacktown. He laughed.

I was still too young to know where I was. I remember a huge building with black, white and red stripes on its roof. There was an emblem on it, with images of Aboriginal men pointing their spears in water. I later learnt it was the Blacktown Workers Club, in whose kitchen I went on to complete my first school work experience: peeling carrots, and eating chicken schnitzel and hot chips smothered in gravy.

Mummy told me I would be starting at a Christian school, and I was upset. I was used to seeing Catholic students in the inner west wearing brown shoes to school. I did not want to wear brown shoes. But my school wasn't Catholic, and Blacktown was cool. We wore black shoes at Tyndale. My school friends were blonde-haired and blue-eyed, had ADD and discussed divorced parents.

At 67 Reservoir Road, my neighbours were Turkish, Chinese, Indian and Filipino. The first time I did karaoke was at my Filipino friend Laura's house. My brother and I used to ride our bikes really fast around the block, straight down the hill, and then down the stairs and in the garden. That was my favourite part. I hated walking my bike back up the hill, though.

Another Ghanaian family lived nearby for a while, but they moved away, to North Sydney. I danced at the daughter's wedding about fifteen years later. She told her mum to tell our cultural dance group not to embarrass her. She was in denial about her heritage and her skin colour. We told our Uncle Yaw that *she* was probably going to embarrass *us* and that we didn't want to perform. Well, we did. Her friends and family loved it and, as we predicted, when we invited her to the dance floor she couldn't dance. We picked up our costumes and left satisfied.

When I was fifteen, my parents built a house. We had to leave 67 Reservoir Road because the owners wanted to move back in, so it was perfect timing for us. While the builders finished our house, we moved to Walters Road, which was much closer and an easier walk to school. Our new neighbours were different: tired, lackadaisical and invisible. They stayed inside most of the time, and we had little interaction.

We came home one day to see the front door open and the neighbours we never saw peering in. We had been robbed. I have never felt such a strong dislike for people I do not know. How can you enter a house and pick and choose items as though it's a supermarket? My favourite Carman CD was in the sound system. They left my flute on the floor in the upstairs hallway, but took the silver necklace from Michael Hill that Sarah gave me for my sixteenth birthday. I was devastated. The Samoans next door said they saw the guy walking out of the front door, dragging the big black bag my mother had bought on our family trip round the world. That bag had carried all the hair products we could get when we got to America – baubles, creams, waxes, combs, weaves and Kanekalon hair to braid with. The Iranian guy next door had run after the man's car, taking down the numberplate. I had prematurely judged my neighbours: they were just as caring as we were; their lives were just different.

I had a crush on a boy named Kwaku. He came over one day with his family, and I cooked lasagne. My béchamel was made from scratch, but Ghanaian girls just weren't his thing.

One morning, I walked downstairs to eat breakfast and watch video clips, but the station was showing the news, with images of a plane flying into a building. I changed the channel only to see the same images, again and again. I arrived at school to the news that the planes had been hijacked, buildings were down in New York and World War III was looming. My friend Emad was half-Palestinian, and I had heard Palestine mentioned, but he looked unfazed as his parents dropped him off at school.

The police never found the guys who came shopping in our house. They traced the car, but it was also stolen and had been abandoned in Dharruk. We never fully cleaned off the dust they used to expose the fingerprints on my chest of drawers.

....

'Oi, look at that guy walking out of the house.'

'What about him?'

'He's white.'

'Yeah, so?'

'The people that live in that house are black!'

Quakers Hill (2002–2017)

When I was ten, I had gone to visit a friend who lived in Quakers Hill for a sleepover. It was one of the first I was allowed to attend. We cut the lyrics to 'The Boy Is Mine' by Brandy and Monica out of a *TV Hits* magazine and fought over who would sing which part. I wanted to be Brandy, of course; *Moesha* was one of my favourite shows.

Later, I remember, we went outside to play in the massive field just across the road. My dad said it was undeveloped land. They called it the Queen's land, as it was not in use for anything in particular. By the time I turned fourteen and my parents drove us to see the foundations of our new home, I realised it was on a portion of the same Queen's land. By 2002, the house was ready.

It was time to enjoy my new room, new neighbours and a whole new life away from Walters Road.

My siblings and I started catching the bus home. Walking through Blacktown Station with my best friend, Aku, and my siblings made me feel so cool. There were so many of us: young people free in the real world after school. We could go to Westpoint Shopping Centre and look around. We could witness fights at the station. We could decide where to get off the bus to shorten or lengthen our time with friends, and our walk home. We met students from other schools and compared uniforms and homework. It was a new leaf of independence and exposure.

There were only about twenty students of African descent at our school. We all knew one another; our parents were friendly or went to the same church and social gatherings. We were still in the habit of nodding or smiling in acknowledgement when we saw another black person in public. You never knew who would report to your parents that they saw you and you didn't mind them.

Then, one day, I saw a young man that I'd never seen before. We got talking, and he asked me for my number! From here on, I started seeing more people of African descent in and around Blacktown and Quakers Hill. The friends I'd grown up with noticed as well. We couldn't figure it out. So many people from countries we'd not yet encountered: Liberia, Sudan, the Congo and Sierra Leone. Suddenly it wasn't so weird to have a guy propose marriage after seeing you at the station once.

Then there was Isaiah. I got a job working at Payless Shoes in Blacktown. He caught the same bus as my siblings and me. He walked into the store one Thursday evening with a man he presented as his uncle. They asked how old I was and advised that he was interested in marrying me. They had no idea what Ghanaian parents would say to such an idea.

'Sorry folks, the workers club is booked out today.'

'No worries, we understand. Thanks, and happy Father's Day!'

'Remember to book ahead of time for any special day: Father's Day, Mother's Day, Sudanese Independence Day.'

....

It's these memories that make me realise that I didn't grow up 'African' in Australia. I grew up Ghanaian, with a strong appreciation for and understanding of Australian mainstream culture. I did not become African until there were too many of us for society to respect our differences and diversity. I did not become African until my friends and peers decided to start using the vague and Americanised term 'African-Australian' to describe themselves, felling the tall trees our parents had planted in one decisive swoop. 'African' connotes homogeneity. When my Ethiopian friend Hannah invited my Ghanaian friends and me to eat injera, her relatives laughed good-naturedly at how we used our hands to eat it, because we are not the same, and we should celebrate and appreciate that.

I am a proud Ghanaian-Australian, and that comes with a story deeper than this, a background, a culture and a contribution that is just as valid and necessary as that from anyone else from the continent.

....

'Your name's Effie? Are you Greek?'

'I'm from Ghana. We give it to girls born on Friday.'

'Oh, thank God I'm speaking to someone Australian. They tried to transfer me to India and the Philippines.'

'Actually, ma'am, we have no offshore call centres. You were speaking to my colleagues right here in Parramatta.'

'What smells like chocolate?'
  'Oh, that's my cocoa butter.'
  'Who wears chocolate on their skin?'
  Laughter.

HORNSBY (2016)

I saw the girls sitting there. Four of them, in blonde hair and school uniforms. As soon as they saw us sitting down with our plastic takeaway containers of sushi, I knew they'd have something to say. 'Africans.' Hair flips. 'Disgusting.'

We finished eating, and with a flick of my braids I walked away. Steaming slowly and calmly like sago pudding on Christmas Day. How I wish I'd written an email to their school. Walked up to them and told them that I had been here longer than they'd been in school. But there is something about being black that empowers and disempowers simultaneously.

By 2016, I had moved to Ghana and was working on my artistic practice there, occasionally coming home to Sydney to be in a play or go on tour. I had left Australia because after visiting Ghana with friends when I was nineteen, I came back to Sydney and had a revelation of where I was. It had suddenly hit me that I no longer knew how to navigate stolen land. I had no idea how to handle racist and ignorant people who made assumptions about who I was.

My mother had advocated for the rights of refugees and women her whole life here, and was given the honour of becoming a Member of the Order of Australia. My father had established himself as the first minister of Ghanaian descent in his church. My brother had achieved amazing things in his career, and my sister was also setting herself up for a powerful legacy.

My family had moved from our home on the field of Quakers Hill into a heritage-listed home. Ghanaians had integrated so seamlessly into Aussie culture, and now we were just Africans.

In Ghana I didn't feel self-aware and tense, knowing that a racially charged remark could be flung at any point in my day.

....

'Fiffi, you can't go to Westpoint for late-night shopping.'

'What? Why not? You've never had a problem before.'

'Because the police are watching out for Sudanese youths. You're tall, you're dark, and they can't tell the difference.'

Lost in Translation

Nasra Hersi

For me, growing up Somali in Australia meant confusion. Literally and metaphorically. Identity was a complex puzzle, with several missing pieces. The first was language. It meant a loss of culture, a loss of kin and a loss of country. My advice for first-generation Somalis my age and younger is to learn to take pride in our mother tongue. Language is what connects our people, old and young. It is the basic building blocks upon which culture is built. With it, we can learn about our history, make sense of our present and build our future.

Hussein Bayahow Afrah was an important person in the community. A sultan of a small tribe. A local camel herder in the town of Wardheer. A dutiful son and a gifted artist. To me, he was simply *awoowe* (grandpa).

My grandfather loved storytelling. He had a knack for it. He was not formally educated, but you would never guess by his impeccable way with words. Some would say he was a natural performer. In particular, he loved poetry, or *gabay*, as it is referred to in Somali.

On occasion, my mother listened intently as an older woman fondly recalled my grandfather performing in the streets of Mogadishu. At dusk, many people would gather to watch *ciyaarta* (performances). *Ciyaarta* was a common social event, where the local young men and women would fraternise, and bond over their love of the performances. The older woman mentioned that even married women would attend to listen to the rising young talent that was Hussein. It was imperative that the women be stealthy. In the 1940s, it was not befitting of a married woman to be seen in that environment. Nevertheless, they ignored social protocol and gazed in awe as my grandfather cleverly tied rhymes together, woven through with alliteration and metaphors.

During his youth, he would regularly travel across cities and recite poetry. He began to be well known – a young man often seen singing his own praises, literally and figuratively. This was because Somali poetry is commonly sung, as part of a performance, rather than delivered as a standard recitation.

MEEL AAN MAY LAGA LISEYN
MADOOBA LAGA RARAYN
MAJERTEEN LAGA AQOON
INAAN MARAY MAOOG TIHIIN

MEEL AAN TAY LAGA LISEYN
TIMO DHEER LALA HADLEEN
HARTIGA TEEL TEEL KU YAHAY
INAAN TAGAY MAOOG TIHIIN

A distant place where she-camels are not milked
Where camels are not used for travel
Where the Majerteen clan is not known
To such a place, I have travelled (would you believe?)

A distant place where she-camels are not milked
Where young women cannot be courted
Where the Harti are few and far
To such a place, I have travelled (would you believe?)

In 1940s Somalia, it was not uncommon for people to be raised in, marry within and grow old in the same village. The people in your locality would know your family, lineage and clan. During this time, Somalia was largely composed of nomadic societies. For such societies, camels were treasured commodities. They offered a source of milk, transport and investment. Thus, a place where camels are not even worth being milked was unfathomable. A place where your clan is not known and your close kinsmen are few and far between – such a place was strange, to say the least.

These lines of poetry were recited by my grandfather after his experiences travelling all over Somalia. He would regularly appear on Radio Mogadishu, a popular radio station, earning the love and respect of the people. This poem describes a young man's worldview expanding.

Decades later, he travelled to Australia, a place where camels are not domesticated. They are not used for milk or for travel. The Majerteen clan or any other Somali clan is obscure.

A distant place where she-camels are not milked
Where camels are not used for travel
Where the Majerteen clan is not known
To such a place, I have travelled (would you believe?)

These words were even more true of his diaspora experience. It is much like the diaspora experience of many other refugees and immigrants.

I wish I could tell you that I have spent endless hours listening to my grandfather recite lyrical art. That, however, would be a lie. Casual conversation was my comfort zone with him. Whenever my grandfather would drift from that and slip into sagacious speech, my shallow knowledge of the language would become apparent.

My grandfather was very complex in the way he spoke. When I was growing up, it made him very difficult to understand. My mother often said he 'spoke in riddles'. I simply could not describe it any better. It was almost as though every other sentence was ambiguous or highly cryptic. Unfortunately, I did not have the keys to unlock the meaning.

It did not help that I was losing my ability to communicate. Once I began school, I would return home each day knowing a little more English and a little less Somali.

I learnt at a young age that it was the norm for Somalis to be brutally honest. This cultural norm has carried through to many Somalis in the diaspora, despite being thousands of kilometres away from home. The assertive ways that were so deeply engrained were bred from generations of nomads who spent their days taming camels. Camels are large and heavy animals, high-maintenance by nature. You won't get anywhere by being meek with them. Years of swelteringly hard labour will surely shape a generation of thick skin and sharp tongues.

Due to this brutal honesty, local people never hesitated to point out that I was losing fluency in my native language. Even my older siblings felt the need to taunt me for every stutter, mispronunciation and improper use of grammar. The days where I was 'good at Somali' began to seem like a vague memory. It's unfortunate, as it led me to second-guess myself every time I strung a sentence together in Somali. I think it was around my early teens when I became uninterested in speaking it altogether.

Somalis have a rich history of poetry. Women would recite famous lines of poetry as they went about their household chores.

Buraanbur (a dance) at weddings would begin with personalised poetry written for the bride and groom, praising them, their respective families and their clans. Senior dignitaries would begin their speeches with poetry. Two clans preparing for battle would each send their best poet to have a showdown before they fought physically. Often, conflict was even resolved through poetry. Poetry is very deeply embedded in the culture – so much so that Somalia is sometimes dubbed 'the nation of poets'.

My grandfather would often worry that his descendants would never be able to listen to and appreciate his poetry. This was a valid concern, as he never recorded his work. This was common among Somali artists. Unlike in the West, which has a culture of documentation, Somalis spread knowledge orally. Interestingly, the Somali language first gained an official alphabet in 1972, but many Somalis can recite songs and poetry that are centuries old.

Much like my grandfather, I naturally took a liking to writing, including poetry. I was six years old when I first encountered poetry. I recall my Grade 1 teacher introducing the concept as 'writing that has rhyming words in it'. I rushed home from school and shoved my first poem under my mother's nose. It was a poem about fruit, and it was very trivial. But she was so proud, so very proud. She gushed over it and showed my entire family. She urged me to continue writing. I was happy to accept every modicum of parental praise my six-year-old attention-seeking self could get. However, I didn't understand why she was so immensely happy. Hindsight is truly 20/20. I no longer need to ask why; I understand.

I recall many instances where my grandfather would ask me to share some of my writing with him. I would remind him that I couldn't write well in Somali. He assured me that he was happy to listen to my English writing.

I never fulfilled his request. I regret that now. At the time, I was very conscious of the fact that I could write fluently in English but not in Somali. I remember feeling very embarrassed. Somehow, I thought it was an indictment on me.

I cannot help but think of all the great memories we could have formed had I not given up my mother tongue. We had a shared love of writing; it is a shame we were not ever able to share it together.

At nineteen, I can now say I understand the importance of learning your native language. I missed the opportunity to connect with my grandfather on a deeper level. I robbed myself of many childhood anecdotes, his invaluable advice and his great wisdoms. Most of all, I missed the chance to hear my grandfather's story from my grandfather himself.

Home

Suban Nur Cooley

To be African in Australia is to be among the drifting diaspora. Nomadic beings who find themselves on an isolated continent through displacement or a disconnection from the umbilical thread of the motherland. Sometimes it's a curious heart or a quest to be closer to the ends of the earth that drives this seeking out of a new home. Other times, it's the fissures created by a civil war that cause a fleeing to somewhere safer, before it becomes a found home. Being African in Australia is, in its essence, a journey unusual.

A SANDY STREET WITH A NAME I CANNOT REMEMBER, MOGADISHU

It was 1987. We were living in a white stone house my parents had bought strategically – it was not far from the airport or from the Indian Ocean. My parents put much of their savings into this home, not knowing that the bleak horror of the 1991 civil war was around the corner, and that in twelve months we would be moving to Australia. This is where we left our childhood memories: as a wad of family photos and videos that sat in a cupboard we planned to return to, but never did.

Departure, Somalia

'Kookaburra sits on the old gum treeeeeee ... '

I don't have many memories from my migratory trip, but I do remember singing the only Australian song I knew on the plane, amid that brightness only found above the clouds, when you're one atmospheric step closer to the sun.

I was eight years old.

Arrival, Australia

Back in Somalia, I delighted in sneaking my sister's *Archie* comics. I'd sit on a sand mound behind our watermelon plants and devour its pages. Though I enjoyed the comic, I loved the M&M and Sea Monkey ads in its pages more. The ads were flamboyant and colourful, and my seven-year-old self wanted nothing more than to eat American candy while watching my Sea Monkeys grow. I can't tell you which airport we flew into when we arrived in Australia, but I can tell you it was the first time I saw a vending machine full of American candy. Now, all I had to do was find my Sea Monkeys.

McCormack Street, Curtin, Canberra

Our house on McCormack sat practically at the centre of the hilly, horseshoe-shaped street. We were immigrants in a new country with no connections, friends or family, and Curtin seemed like the most idyllic setting to start afresh.

In my time there, Curtin became many things to me. It was where I learnt to develop a love of nature, and a fascination with cicada shells. I'd see them stuck on gum trees and collect them for examination, puzzled by the ridiculous amount of detail invested in what wasn't a living creature, but the manifestation of its perfect shedding. How could something so precise be a shell? So empty of life? And in that house, I understood the word 'façade', without yet knowing it. I understood it was a 'showing', not a 'being'.

Curtin was also where I began to understand what racism was, through my experiences at the primary school. My closest friend was a half-Indian, half-English girl named Claire who collected chocolate Easter eggs to decorate her room, because she was vegan and couldn't eat them. We were the brownest kids in the playground. Together, we didn't feel alone. I only felt lonely when other kids at Curtin Primary misplaced their things. Those items were assumed stolen – by me, of course. An eight-colour ballpoint pen became my scarlet letter. The only incriminating evidence was that I had one when Virginia had lost hers. Clearly, the black immigrant girl had to have stolen it, because how could she have one of her own? To these Australian kids, I was a cicada shell – no innards worth discovering, just a manifestation of what they chose to see of me.

McNicoll Street, Hughes, Canberra

I only have two memories of our time at McNicoll. I remember my brother riding a tricycle in the yard. Up and down the driveway he went, until my parents bought a vintage mint-teal Austin Devon that took up his riding space. It was also the first place I remember celebrating Christmas.

As we were Muslims, Christmas wasn't a staple holiday. Moving to Australia changed that, as our family made friends and we culturally adapted to the gift-giving, while they accommodated us with halal options at Aussie barbeques. Our friends were also mostly other African families: South Africans, Kenyans, Eritreans, Tanzanians, Zimbabweans, Somalis, Ghanaians.

In Canberra in the 1980s and 1990s, Africa was a country. We had African parties at community centres, where the adults danced to their favourite tunes from the continent, while the children played together in and around the space. We ate *so good*: sambusa, jollof rice, mandazi, biryani, fufuo, injera and zigni and much, much more. In Canberra, our pan-Africanism shone. The communities were all too small to self-segregate, so we celebrated together, intertwined in our collective connectedness as an African diaspora living in Australia.

In this collective connectedness, I met Penina. My first best friend. Half-Australian, half-Tanzanian, she was taller than me, two years younger, and the only friend in whose house I was allowed to sleep over. Most of my summers were spent with her family, making memories on Mortlock Circuit; driving to the South Coast to read *Dolly* magazines and trying to mix mud masks; eating chicken-salted chips from the local shops.

KITCHENER STREET, HUGHES, CANBERRA

Kitchener was the first house to become my home. It was ours, purchased by my parents on a large corner lot on a busy road in Hughes. We were in walking distance from everything we needed, even the hospital. Our next-door neighbours, the Gregorys, had a pool in their backyard with a gate to access it from ours. Alpha was Canadian, and Gordon grew up in England. Their children had names as weird as ours: Tauri, Pella, Tadryn and Parri. The gate connecting our house to their backyard was a metaphor for their openness towards our family. I also fondly remember the elderly couple across the road, because they gifted us old Repco bikes from the 1970s. My brother and I traversed most of the streets in Hughes with them, blazing down hills with our arms above our heads, eyes squinting against the sun. Hughes was what I wanted all of Australia to be.

In the mid-1990s, my mother applied to sponsor my aunt and her children to move to Australia. My aunt Feyruz, my *habaryar*, was like a second mother to me, as she had spent much of her youth caring for us. The war in Somalia was getting worse and, thankfully, her refugee status was accepted. When she arrived with her two sons, we finally had blood family up the street, in Garran.

Hughes was also the home of Carroll Street: subsidised housing where many international graduate students attending the Australian National University lived. At Hughes Primary School, I had black and brown friends from around the world. The playground became a haven for the herds. We hopscotched in turns, played Bull Rush by the hedges and jump-roped with joyful faces that showed we had no idea our playtime was ephemeral. It was also back when religious studies at school only focused on Christian teaching, so me, Azka and Mohamed would be excused during that hour to play together in a separate room.

We stayed in our house on Kitchener well into my high-school years. By Year 10, I had solidified friendships that I knew would last my lifetime. That's when my parents decided it was time for us to move to Melbourne, to be around more Somalis. I was heartbroken. Starting afresh when I felt so grounded seemed like the worst idea ever. For my going-away party, me and some of my closest friends sneaked into the golf course behind my house to have a water-balloon fight. It was one of the most memorable nights of my life.

My teenage remorse was evident, and my aunt Feyruz offered to let me stay with her in Canberra. My parents were having none of it. This was as close to *dhaqan celis* as we could get, living in Australia. A return to Somali culture via a city with a larger diaspora.

BRYSON COURT, BUNDOORA, MELBOURNE

Bryson Court was a multicultural cul-de-sac on the outskirts of metropolitan Melbourne (outskirts in those days, anyway). Directly across the street from us lived the Steenvelds, a beautiful coloured South African family with a boy and a girl: Emile was about three years younger than me, and Joy was two years older. I recall walking awkwardly across the street to introduce myself to Emile while he played basketball in front of his house. I tripped, and we still both make fun of me over it to this day. Paul Rajkovski lived down at the end of the cul-de-sac, and the three of us would walk to catch the tram to school together.

Making friends at the cliquey Bundoora Secondary College in Year 11 seemed like the sort of challenge the protagonist in a young-adult novel would face. Some of these high-schoolers had known one another since kindergarten. There's no way to compete with that kind of connection. And so, the newbies became besties. Me and Elena, a Cyprian who also started at the school that year, became inseparable. We were both less interested in getting dolled up and more interested in being tomboys in our teenage sets of Kappa and Adidas (because Bundoora is a suburb that was predominantly Macedonian, Greek and Italian). Of course, we liked boys who didn't like us back. There were reasons. Some overt, some covert.

The Melbourne Somali community was growing in the mid-1990s due to the war, and with that growth, my closest friends no longer became those I met at school but people who understood what it meant to be Australian and Somali at the same time. My ride-or-die, Deman, was a Somali Sujuu girl living with her aunt in Preston. We were inseparable. We put relaxers in our hair together while binging on horror movies. She introduced me to sushi and plucked my eyebrows for the first time when she decided to become a beautician. We'd catch buses and trams to get to the Carlton highrises to hang out with other Somali teens. There, we had our first real crushes at dance parties while singing the lyrics to Next's 'Too Close' or Brandy and Monica's 'The Boy Is Mine'. The problem was, Somali boys back then weren't really into the girls who danced at parties singing along to 'Too Close'.

Though our friendship was fleeting, Deman and I couldn't see it then. As far as we knew, we were growing old together, and would maybe raise our kids back in Africa someday. But time had other plans.

One day, my mother came home and announced that my sister and I had a new Somali friend to meet. She had no sisters her age, and when she met my mother, she loved her so much she asked if she had daughters. 'Two, in fact!' my mother exclaimed. And so, Fahima came over one day, and became instant family. She was also the first in my friendship group to get a job when we were teens. She worked at the Bourke Street McDonald's, and we'd meet her there all the time for free meals before the end of her shift. We'd get her in trouble, this rowdy crew of young Somali women, loitering around one of the busiest Maccas in Melbourne. Though we didn't get drunk together, or get into the conventional teenage trouble, we still went adventuring on Melbourne's public transport systems, finding new pockets of the city and making memories. We'd go to see late-night movies at the cinema in Crown Casino, take half a day to get to St Kilda for sunset pics and make it back to Oriole Road in Heidelberg in time for treats at the Somali mall. For Somali weddings, we would don our best *diracs*, go to Sydney Road to get our hair pressed, wear our mother's *dahab*, and do our makeup, ready to dance and flirt with our futures.

High Street, Preston, Melbourne

Just after I finished high school, my mother's penchant for cooking became her passion. She decided to open up a spice shop in Preston, and we took residence above it. There was some charm to the place, in the way that old buildings in Melbourne often have charm: high ceilings to make up for cramped space, a tiny concrete backyard and direct access to the Bell Street train station, which was a two-minute walk from our garage. The spice shop was called Nourrain's. My parents had painted the interior of the shop and upstairs in what I call 'immigrant chic': Pepto-Bismol pink with a mint-green trim. Likely colours that were on sale at Bunnings when they went paint shopping.

By the time we lived on High Street, the internet occupied a giant space in the lives of my siblings and me. My brother Faarah and I were Napster junkies, downloading all kinds of songs to enjoy on our parents' desktop on the ground floor of the shop: Destiny's Child, Mystikal, 702, Jill Scott, Dru Hill, Erykah Badu, Outkast, Jagged Edge – we were RnB and hip-hop aficionados. We also got into a computer game called *Drugwars*. I have no idea how we came across it, but our *Mario Brothers* and *Donkey Kong* days were over. Instead we'd shout, 'Did you invest in cocaine when the market changed?' and my dad would frown at us from over his coffee and newspaper in the kitchen. My older sister, who had always been too cool for us, would mock us whenever she'd come over, pregnant and newly hijabed since getting married.

I was also falling in love with an American I'd met online, before it was a thing to meet people online. His name was Caleb, and he visited while we were living in High Street. In the time he was in Melbourne, we took road trips, had typical couple fights and connected profoundly. My parents had yet to warm to the idea of him, but he was present, and our relationship was seemingly getting more serious.

Gunyan Place, Ngunnawal, Canberra

In 2002, I moved to Canada to work in a coffee shop in a Torontonian subway. Of course, I did this partially to be closer to my American boo, Caleb, who lived in Michigan. Being in Toronto meant I was a five-hour drive from him, and our relationship flourished. But while I was in Canada, nourishing a life abroad and a budding romance, my aunt Feyruz died in her sleep. And though I couldn't make it home in time for her funeral, I moved back to Australia sooner than I had planned.

My parents moved back to Canberra to support my uncle Abdullahi, who was now a single father caring for two young sons and two-year-old twin daughters. They sold our house on Kitchener and bought a brand-new house in Ngunnawal, on the outskirts of Canberra. For long-time residents of Canberra, Cockington Green was once the outskirts of Canberra, and my bus drove fifteen minutes past it to get me home. I had transferred from RMIT to the University of Canberra, and I got a job at the Optus shop in the Belconnen mall to help around the house. Though I wanted move out, Somali women don't move out of their homes until they're married. So, I was back at home, busy trying to figure out my future while supporting my family in the ways I knew how.

My father was given a job opportunity in Dubai, so my brother and I were left to our own devices for almost a year. In this time, our reliance on each other grew as we took care of the house, paying utilities and hanging out together with our friends.

I was struggling with my deepening love for Caleb, and how little he fit into my Somali-Australian world. While my parents were away, Caleb came to stay in our house in Ngunnawal for three months. By the end of that period, we pretty much knew we were going to get married, but we didn't know how to approach the subject with our families: he was a white Christian American, and I was a black Somali-Australian. Sometimes the best approach is simply denial. So, in 2004, we got engaged.

BRITTEN AVENUE, LANSING, MICHIGAN

Today, I'm thirty-seven years old. I live in a place that a dear friend aptly named 'swirl city' for how many mixed-race couples and children reside here (turns out, more than anywhere else in the United States!). I sometimes swap the word 'holiday' for 'vacation' because I've lived in America for more than eleven years, and the only Africans who aren't American I meet are the friends I have made in graduate school while working on my PhD. In America, I am just black. I'm not an immigrant, not Somali, not Muslim, not Australian. Short of wearing a hijab, there's no way to hint at my identity or my past, other than my disappearing accent. I miss the nuances that my identity held in Australia. What I don't miss is Australia's denial that racism is a problem, and our inability to accept that we have as much work to do as America does. We may not have the same gun problem, but the violence and hatred is shared.

I sat in my parents' home in Reservoir on my last trip home, appalled by the rhetoric the Australian media were using to talk about Africans in Australia. As I consider moving back to raise my child, I dream of an Australia equipped to support his nuanced identities. Growing up African in Australia is like growing up African anywhere else, but on the islands or on the continent: it means feigning a sense of black futurity, and hoping it materialises.

Four Stages

Rafeif Ismail

Two months ago, my paternal grandfather passed away. It was a Wednesday, usually my favourite day of the week – now always a reminder that it has been (x) days since he left us. The worst thing about grief is the forgetting: those split-second eternities when you are caught between dreaming and waking. Those moments in between heartbeats, as you draw in a breath, before it leaves your body with a sob. The space of a step when suddenly the weight of memories makes you stumble. I still forget there is a gaping hole in the universe in the shape of his smile.

My grandfather, my Baba Jidu, as I'd called him ever since I could speak, was not my first family member to pass away. He was not even the first grandparent – my maternal grandmother died in 2009, and ten years of grief lines have yet to fade from my mother's face, but she moves forward because that's what Black women do.

Grief in exile is a funny thing. There is no 'closure'; there is no room to contemplate the enormity of the loss. Often you're too busy consoling everyone else, making arrangements, keeping up a façade of normality.

Grief in exile is complicated, because it's hard to know exactly what you're grieving for.

1. Shock

The day we run is like every other day. The adhan carries through the town, calling people to prayer. My mother wakes and waters the plants, makes breakfast and packs our backpacks. We leave our house as though we're just going to visit relatives. We do visit relatives. My younger brothers are a toddler and an infant, and I'm nearly six years old as I hug my maternal grandmother for the last time, as my oldest *khalo*, maternal uncle, cries. All of our goodbyes are filled with tears. We get into a white truck with only the clothes on our backs and a few possessions, some photo albums. My father travels separately; he joins us in Khartoum.

When we get to Cairo, it's a whole new world. I taste apples for the first time: sweet, and slightly overripe, but not so much that they have lost their crunch. Apples become my favourite food, though I miss the taste of fresh sugarcane and guava, the taste of home.

We thought it would be a year, maybe two, before we could go back home. In Cairo I have the same dream every night for months, of walking down a new street, turning a corner and finding myself near my family home, of hearing the clamour of voices, a cacophony of chatter, singing, debate and laughter.

I had never been outside Sudan, never seen people with skin paler than Nile soil, never thought my Arabic was not Arabic, never doubted who I was and how I was, until Egypt. Years later, I find out that my paternal great-grandmother thought her husband was a ghost lost in the desert the first time she saw him: the brown-skinned Turkish soldier who deserted his post during the occupation and fell in love in the land his people conquered. I wonder if my late grandfather had questions about his identity, if he ever wanted to know his father's homeland, what he thought about being born in a country under occupation. I will never get to ask those questions.

My grief is mixed with anger, to have lost nearly a lifetime that could have been spent with family. Seventeen years of knowing family, learning language, learning history and culture, learning self, gone. To have had seventeen years *stolen* from my family is a wound I will always carry. The blame lies at the feet of the Bashir dictatorship, alongside the bodies of loved ones lost or buried, alongside villages and towns, burnt; so many lives and lifetimes, stolen. The blame lies at the feet of every single person who benefited from the exploitation of Black lands and Black lives. The spectre of pre-colonial Sudan is not far from my life – my eldest *amo*, paternal uncle, was born four years after independence. Most of the elders in my family, in my country, spent the majority of their lives in lands occupied. It's hard to find an identity in the midst of all that confusion. It's even harder when elements of your identity seem conflicting at first glance.

In Australia, the question I get asked the most is, 'Where are you from?' In other words, explain why you are Black, and existing in this space. Or, more rarely, 'I hope to find a common connection.'

Most conversations go like this:

'Where are you from?'

'Perth.'

'Where are you really from?'

'Sudan.'

'But you don't look Sudanese.'

'But you can't be Sudanese.'

'But you're not really Sudanese.'

There is no single way that all Sudanese people look, act or speak. Just as Blackness is not monolithic. The homogenisation of

Sudanese people further erases cultural and ethnic groups that have been purposely written out of our collective history. Genocide isn't just about the violence; it thrives on the silence around it.

In my first year of 'mainstream' school in Australia, after the intensive English centres deemed my progress in the language satisfactory, 'Where are you from?' was the first question my teacher asked me, before even knowing my name.

Around that time, I began to learn a universal truth: Black girls are seen as women before they are children, objects before they are human. 'Growing up' isn't an option when you are already grown in the eyes of the world. A school uniform does not protect you from white women touching you without consent as you're walking down the road. It does nothing to stop the gazes of older white men following you, or comments about how 'well developed' you are. A school uniform does not protect you from the idea that, for you, the ages twelve, fourteen and sixteen are not 'too young'. That then you are 'old enough'.

As an adult, I am very particular about my personal space; I cannot stand being close to people, and I am always hyper-vigilant in crowds. Being able to say 'no' and 'don't touch me' have been the most liberating things about the last few years – there are indignities adults will inflict on a Black girl child, especially in public, that they wouldn't dare with someone who can speak back. I relish being able to take the train without using a schoolbag as an insufficient shield, and to stand in spaces without trying to make myself small. I love being able to speak with friends and know that they respect my space and boundaries. For the first time in my life, I do not blame or despise my body, having realised that every instance of violence inflicted, whether macro or micro aggression, was not my fault.

2. Guilt

How do you live with yourself when you are alive while so many are dead or dying? There is survivor's guilt when you make it to a new country. Knowing that people around you sacrificed, and were prepared to sacrifice, their lives, their world, for your survival is a heavy burden. The only difference between me and the people imprisoned in offshore detention is luck. If that white truck had been stopped, if the security forces had raided our house again the night before, or just after we left, if my father had been stopped before boarding the plane, things could have gone differently. A billion possibilities of what could have gone wrong still go through my mind. It is luck that has us treated as marginally more human than our siblings of circumstance in onshore and offshore detention.

In 2017, I went back to my first primary school here, an intensive English centre where some teachers discouraged me from speaking Arabic. I was supposed to speak to students, to somehow 'inspire' them. As I stood in the front of the room, I felt too old and far too young to be in this position. A blink of an eye ago, I was sitting in the same spot, picking up every third word in English and thinking that adults had all the answers, waiting to feel safe or saved. But at that age, I had not seen anyone who looked like me, spoke like me, lived like me.

My first question to this group of children was, 'What's your favourite superhero, and why?'

They had a multitude of answers to the whos, but the whys were pretty similar:

'Because I want to change the world.'

'Because I want to make my family safe.'

'Because I want to help save people.'

'Because I want to be brave.'

Children of diasporic heritage are aware of the reality of the world around them. Not understanding something and being unable to communicate your understanding are completely different things. We rarely give an opportunity to those who are affected the most by the life-altering circumstances of migration, forced or otherwise, to speak or find a common language.

My favourite superheroes growing up were *Superman* and *Wonder Woman*. They were both far away from home. They couldn't return, yet they tried to make a better world where they were. Comics were the only commonality I could find between Egypt and Australia, and I would sit and read them day after day, during recess and lunch. It's how I learnt to read English. In those early years, I imagined myself an alien abandoned on a foreign planet. I would daydream about Amazons teaching me how to defend myself, about finding people who could understand what I could not yet put into words. About returning home.

3. RAGE

'Don't open the doors to strangers,' my mother warns. My father tells me to make sure all the lights and the televisions are on. They're only leaving for two hours, yet I double- and triple-check every lock in the house, close every curtain, and wait. This is Australia, 2018. We have been here for fourteen years.

Late at night, when I am unable to sleep due to stress or distress, I walk around my house. I look into my siblings' rooms, look in on my parents, to make sure they are okay. I check every lock in the house – twice, three times, and again, until my thoughts stop racing. There are occasions when I hear a noise in the backyard and stay awake until dawn, counting the exits, the distance to the front door, how long it would take to break the windows. Should I text my siblings to run? Back home, if you were sleeping inside, you heard the *thump, thump* of the Kalashnikovs on the shoulders of soldiers before they broke down the door, if you were lucky. If you weren't, you'd wake up with the rifles pointed at your family. In Sudan, we slept under the stars. Every night, my parents would drag our mattress out into the courtyard, put my siblings and me between them and shield us even in sleep. Noises meant raids, meant disappearances, meant strangers. They meant pretending to sleep, practising that instinctual *if I don't see them, they cannot see me.*

I still freeze when I wake up, to listen and wait. There are times when cars backfire, and I duck for cover. Every time someone reaches into their jacket, my heartbeat spikes. I steel myself with every ring of the phone or knock at our door. We fled the war seventeen years ago, but the war hasn't left us.

Once, after speaking at an event, I was thanked for my 'inspiring' and 'articulate' speech. It was not the first time this had happened, but it was the first time my response was not something that somewhat rhymed with 'thank you'. I was angry, in public, for the first time, because I was being cast into the mould of 'model refugee'. My life was being used as a tool to assuage white guilt – to provide absolution even as my across-the-world siblings and I struggle through the shackles of white supremacy. My experience and existence are not teachable moments for those who can step in and out of power. We escape wars just to end up bound by different chains.

4. (Re)Building

With the death of my grandfather came the death of a dream. You see, I had always thought that one day I'd go back home. It has been seventeen years since I stepped foot on Sudanese soil, but there was always a part of me that believed we would go back after it became safe. There was always a part of me waiting to complete a childhood there. That part waited and waited and waited, even as hope crumbled with each passing year, with each grave of a family member or of a friend who might as well have been family. With each act of violence.

That part persisted somehow – a dam to keep at bay a flood that has been gathering since I was five years old – and with this last death, my grandfather's, the dam has shattered and I am left trying to wade through torrents of grief and rage.

Sudan was family, it was laughter, it was never being alone, it was being blanketed by unconditional love. It was the scent of *bakhoor*, the taste of sugarcane and guava, the lanterns lighting the street during Ramadan. It was Mustafa Said Ahmed's music and Mahjoub Sharif's poetry. It was also police cars at our doors, in front of our school. It was the marks of lashings across my father's back, relatives in hiding, being spoken of in code. My mother risking her life again and again for her children. It was like living in the middle of a storm, praying to not be hit by the debris.

Egypt was a flood of change, unexpected and terrifying – a deluge that carried us all the way to Australia.

I'm still trying to figure out what Australia is.

It has now been (x) days since my grandfather passed away. I go through the motions each day, and try not to regret what I have lost. I am learning, slowly, that grief does not dwindle by the day, but that the capacity to deal with it expands.

As I write this it has been 6210 days since I was last home. And I am still trying to find a way to exist in this world.

I have spent 5294 days in Australia, and I am finally learning to grow into myself.

Contributors

THE EDITORS

Maxine Beneba Clarke is a widely published Australian writer of Afro-Caribbean descent. She is the author of the multi-award-winning story collection *Foreign Soil*, which has been set on high-school curriculums; the memoir *The Hate Race*, which won the NSW Premier's Literary Award – Multicultural; the poetry collection *Carrying the World*, which won the 2017 Victorian Premier's Award for Poetry; and the children's book *The Patchwork Bike*, a 2017 CBCA Honour Book.

Magan Magan is a writer and poet who has read work at the National Gallery of Victoria, the National Young Writers' Festival, the Emerging Writers' Festival and Melbourne Writers Festival. His work has been published in *Cordite Poetry Review* and the anthologies *Shots from the Chamber*, *Australian Poetry* and *Contemporary Australian Feminist Poetry*. Magan's latest book is *From Grains to Gold* (2018).

Ahmed Yussuf is a writer and journalist whose work has featured in *Acclaim Magazine*, *The Guardian*, TRT World and Jalada Africa. He was also an artist in the 2018 Digital Writers Festival. He co-founded the race and politics podcast *Race Card*.

THE CONTRIBUTORS

Faustina Agolley is a television host, an actor, a DJ, a producer and a writer. She has hosted *Video Hits*, *The Voice* and *The Sydney Gay and Lesbian Mardi Gras*. She made her stage debut in the Molière award-winning play *The Father*, and toured Australia and New Zealand as Oprah Winfrey's resident DJ on her 'An Evening with Oprah' tour. Faustina is a graduate of Media and Communications at the University of Melbourne and Media Studies at RMIT University.

Adut Wol Akec is a South Sudanese–born Australian writer and poet who lives in Naarm (Melbourne). She has a Bachelor of Science, majoring in environmental management. In 2018 she was an inaugural recipient of the Next Chapter grant for developing writers.

Prue Axam was born and grew up in Sydney, and has also lived in Kyoto, Japan and on the west coast of the United States. She studied English literature and art history and theory at the University of Sydney, and she now continues to live and work in Sydney with her partner and young daughter.

Candy Bowers is a radical theatre-maker, director, lyricist, playwright, actor, teacher and filmmaker. She has starred on screen and stage across the country, and her original plays include *Hot Brown Honey*, *Australian Booty*, *Sista She*, *One the Bear* and *Twelve* (a soul musical from the streets after William Shakespeare's *Twelfth Night*).

Santilla Chingaipe is an award-winning journalist and filmmaker. She spent nearly a decade working for *SBS World News*, which saw her report from across Africa and interview some of the continent's prominent leaders. Her work explores contemporary migration, cultural identities and politics. Santilla is currently developing several factual and narrative projects. She writes regularly for *The Saturday Paper* and is a member of the federal government's Advisory Group on Australia–Africa Relations.

Suban Nur Cooley is an Australian writer and poet of Somali descent living in the United States, where she is pursuing a doctoral degree in rhetoric and writing. Her research focuses on women of the Somali diaspora and how their identity performance is affected by memory, migration/displacement and assimilation.

Muma Doesa, MC and vocalist, was the first Australian-born in her family after they left South Africa to escape apartheid. Muma began performing with her all-female crew, Ladies Luv Hip Hop. She released 'Muma Doesa's Mixtape Marinade' in 2009, her debut album, *Ms Fortune*, in 2013 and 'Don Muma Mixtape' in 2018. Muma has performed in various venues in Australia and New York, collaborated with Psycho Les of The Beatnuts and G.E.D., and DJ'd with Quashani Bahd supporting Sister Nancy.

Sara El Sayed is an Egyptian-born Master of Fine Arts student living in Brisbane. Her research focus is digital storytelling by migrant Egyptian women. Her work, both fiction and nonfiction, is influenced by her culture, her family and her identity as a migrant.

Carly Findlay is an award-winning author, speaker and appearance activist, writing on disability and appearance diversity issues. Her first book, a memoir called *Say Hello*, was released in January 2019. She is also editing *Growing Up Disabled in Australia* with Black Inc. Carly has appeared on ABC TV's *You Can't Ask That* and organised the history-making Access to Fashion – a Melbourne Fashion Week event featuring disabled models. She has a Masters of Communication and a Bachelor of eCommerce.

Kamara Gray is the artistic director of Artistry Youth Dance, and is an experienced dance artist, teacher and choreographer. She lectures regularly at schools, colleges and universities, and has worked throughout the United Kingdom, Australia and Kuwait. Her choreographer and performer credits include film, television and live events.

Daniel Haile-Michael was a lead applicant in a 2013 Federal Court racial discrimination case against Victoria Police. He is the co-author (with

Maki Issa) of 'The More Things Change, the More They Stay the Same', a 2015 report exploring racial profiling of the African-Australian community.

Nasra Hersi is a nineteen-year-old writer of Somali descent based in Melbourne. Her work explores themes of identity, migration and family.

Rafeif Ismail is a multilingual writer based in Western Australia and the winner of the 2017 Deborah Cass Prize for Writing. Her work has been published by Margaret River Press, Fremantle Press, *Mascara Literary Review*, *Kill Your Darlings* and Djed Press.

Shona Kambarami is a proud 'difficult woman'. She's been described as 'opinionated', 'argumentative', 'stubborn' and 'loud'. She's an unrepentant intersectional feminist in a patriarchal world, motivated by a desire for social equality for marginalised people. She's a frustrated women's health doctor angered by the racist foundations of Western medicine. She is a writer.

Keenan MacWilliam is a multidisciplinary artist based in Brooklyn, New York. Her work centres on providing a voice to the 'other', using her experience as an adopted, biracial queer woman from Canada as a literal and figurative lens into society and the respective people she's spotlighting.

Kirsty Marillier is a South African actor and writer based in Melbourne. A mixed-race woman of colour, she uses her writing to reclaim her identity and deconstruct the relationship people of colour have with migration and disempowerment. Kirsty trained at the Western Australian Academy of Performing Arts and has performed in a number of plays, including *Coma Land* with the Black Swan Theatre Company. She is currently developing her first original stage play, *Orange Thrower*, and performing in the Australian premiere of *Harry Potter and the Cursed Child*.

Hope Mathumbu is a queer black South African–born woman, who has lived and worked on the sovereign lands of the Kulin Nation since 2003. Her work in public health, radio, arts and various other community development sectors is driven by her belief in the Black African humanist philosophy of Ubuntu.

Tariro Mavondo is a Zimbabwean-born artist raised in Melbourne. Her body of work spans disciplines including acting, writing, performance and consultation. Tariro is an award-winning poet and has appeared in many Australian stage productions, including for the Melbourne and Sydney theatre companies and the Bell Shakespeare Company. She has also appeared in *Neighbours* and *Winners & Losers*, the internationally acclaimed web series *Shakespeare Republic* and the award-winning short film *Arrivals*. Tariro has been a voice-over artist for La Trobe University, the AFL women's league and *Thomas the Tank Engine*.

Guido Melo is an Afro-Brazilian living in Melbourne. He is a photography enthusiast, a digital marketing and social media manager, a part-time writer, a passionate advocate for racial equality and an active member of Melbourne's political and social scene.

Vulindlela Mkwananzi (Vuli) is a music producer, saxophonist, DJ and multidisciplinary artist based between Berlin and Sydney. Vuli has toured around Australia and internationally, including through Europe and Southern Africa. This year and beyond will see Vuli travelling the globe and sharing his positive high-energy music with the world.

Cath Moore is of Afro-Caribbean heritage and has lived in Scotland, America and Belgium. An award-winning screenwriter and filmmaker, Cath tutors in creative writing at the University of Melbourne, is a regular contributor to *The Age* and has written for *SBS Life*, *The Huffington Post* and *The Pin*. She is also a published academic and holds a PhD in Danish screenwriting practices.

Lauren Mullings co-produces the Jamaican Music & Food Festival, which celebrates music and food of Jamaican origin. She also runs a marketing company, Cleverb!tch, which is on a mission to improve the representation of people of colour in the Australian media.

Effie Nkrumah (Benumah) is an interdisciplinary artist and poet of Ghanaian descent brought up in Sydney, Australia. She has worked creatively between Sydney, Accra and New York, granting her a unique sense of humour, aesthetic and keen observation. She holds an MA in Arts Politics from New York University.

Nyadol Nyuon is a commercial litigator and community advocate. She was born in Ethiopia and raised in Kenya, and moved to Australia at age eighteen. In 2011 and 2014, Nyadol was nominated as one of the 100 most influential African-Australians. She is a board member of the Melbourne Social Equity Institute and appears regularly in the media, including on ABC's *The Drum* and *Q&A*.

Tinashe Pwiti is a Zimbabwean-born writer whose stories advocate for women who have suffered domestic abuse or violence, as she is a survivor. She's also passionate about writing stories that raise awareness around suicide prevention and mental-health issues.

Iman Sissay is an eighteen-year-old student based in Tasmania. She lives at home as one of a big, loving family of eight. She feels a great sense of peace when surrounded by close friends and family. She has a deep interest in social issues and is always eager to learn and improve.

Inez Trambas lives in Melbourne and is an editor, a visual artist and a bookworm who is passionate about all things literature and in how we use words to liberate ourselves. In 2017 she founded Negro Speaks of Books, an online platform created to host conversations about books written by authors of colour.

Imam Nur Warsame, born in Somalia and based in Melbourne, is Australia's only openly gay imam. He has a deep knowledge of Islamic scripture (he is one of the few to memorise the entire Qur'an in Arabic), and uses this knowledge to challenge conservative interpretations of Islamic texts. Through his support group, Marhaba, he helps queer Muslim people to reconcile their faith and sexuality or gender. In 2017, the Monette-Horwitz Trust in the United States awarded his significant contributions towards eradicating homophobia.

Khalid Warsame is a writer and arts worker. He is a creative producer at Footscray Community Arts Centre. His short fiction and essays have appeared in a number of publications, and he was recently awarded a Wheeler Centre Hot Desk Fellowship.

Grace Williams is a passionate human-rights activist who believes in the power of stories to bring about change. She is a writer and a student of law, politics, economics and philosophy. She is also the director of human-rights advocacy group Citizen and a lover of Tasmanian wilderness.

Jafri Katagar Alexander X is a social worker, humanitarian and an anti-racism campaigner. After experiencing racism and discrimination at a dental hospital in Melbourne, he started conducting the 'STOP RAC-ISM NOW' campaign at Flinders Street Station to raise awareness about racism in Australia. He participated in the 2017 Parliamentary Inquiry into Migrant Settlement Outcomes, and helped in the making of the SBS documentary *Is Australia Racist?*.

Manal Younus is an Australian-based storyteller from Eritrea whose work explores themes of identity and perseverance. Manal has performed around the country, including at the Sydney Opera House, and presented in many forums, including at the TEDxAdelaide conference, the Adelaide Festival of Ideas, the National Multicultural Women's Conference and George Town Literary Festival in Malaysia. She facilitates workshops for schools, and has appeared on the ABC's *Q&A*. Her book is *Reap* (2015).

Sefakor Aku Zipli is a mother and a practising solicitor in Sydney. She holds degrees in law, writing and cultural studies. She has written and performed a number of spoken-word pieces with a particular focus on the diasporan African experience. Outside her love of words, her interests include watching left-of-centre documentaries with her husband, Matthew, and working with young people in her church youth group.

Publication Details

Sections of Maxine Beneba Clarke's introduction first appeared in 'Black History Month', *The Saturday Paper*, 24 February 2018.

Khalid Warsame's 'Idle Thoughts' first appeared on the Wheeler Centre website, 27 April 2016.

Guido Melo's 'The Long Way Home', Jafri Katagar Alexander X's 'Street Activism', Tinashe Pwiti's 'Di Apprentice' and Inez Trambas's 'Negro Speaks of Books' are transcribed and edited from interviews with Maxine Beneba Clarke, 2018.

A version of Carly Findlay's 'Complex Colour' first appeared in her memoir, *Say Hello*, HarperCollins, 2019.

A version of Candy Bowers' 'Dear Australia, I Love You But …' was published on the General Thinking YouTube channel, https://www.youtube.com/watch?v=yYwOS1mHnfA

Daniel Haile Michael's 'Profiled' is transcribed and edited from an interview with Ahmed Yussuf that first appeared on *TRT WORLD*, June 2018.

Tariro Mavondo's 'The Danger of a Single Story' first appeared in *Overland*, no. 206, Autumn 2012.

Imam Nur Warsame's 'Marhaba' is transcribed and edited from an interview, 2018.

Acknowledgements

A heart-swelling thank you to our families and communities, and to all contributors to *Growing Up African in Australia*, for sharing their stories with such bravery, enthusiasm and generosity. Your words, and your work, make this book the triumph we truly believe it is.

Thanks to the team at Black Inc. for their unwavering support in this endeavour. In particular: Julia Carlomagno, Erin Sandiford, Chris Feik, Kate Nash, Sophy Williams, Marian Blythe, Elisabeth Young and Morry Schwartz.

Our sincere appreciation to Ernest Price, for writing such thoughtful and thorough teacher's notes; to Louise Whelan, for the use of the cover photographs; to Kim Ferguson, for the cover design; and to Thomas Deverall and Akiko Chan for the text design. How beautifully you have dressed our words.

Thank you to the Australian writers of colour who graced the page before us: your footsteps steady our footing.